The care
of creation

Richard Bauckham

Calvin B. DeWitt

Susan Drake Emmerich

Timothy Dudley-Smith

Ron Elsdon

John Guillebaud

Peter Harris

John T. Houghton

Alister E. McGrath

I. Howard Marshall

Jürgen Moltmann

Michael S. Northcott

Oliver M. T. O'Donovan

Ghillean T. Prance

Stephen Rand

Ronald J. Sider

Howard J. Van Till

Lynn White, Jr

Loren Wilkinson

Richard T. Wright

The care
of creation

Focusing concern and action

Editor **R. J. Berry**

Inter-Varsity Press

INTER-VARSITY PRESS
38 De Montfort Street, Leicester LE1 7GP, England

First published 2000

British Library Cataloguing in Publication Data
A catalogue record for this book is available from the British Library.

ISBN 0–85111–657–4

Set in Minion Condensed
Typeset in Great Britain
Printed and bound in Great Britain by Creative Print and Design (Wales), Ebbw Vale

Inter-Varsity Press is the book-publishing division of the Universities and Colleges Christian Fellowship (formerly the Inter-Varsity Fellowship), a student movement linking Christian Unions in universities and colleges throughout Great Britain, and a member movement of the International Fellowship of Evangelical Students. For more information about local and national activities write to UCCF, 38 De Montfort Street, Leicester LE1 7GP.

Contents

Foreword

In May 1999 I was privileged to take part in a day conference in Nairobi on 'Christians and the Environment'. Sharing the platform with me were Cal DeWitt of Au Sable Institute and Peter Harris of A Rocha International, both of whom are contributors to this volume. Participants that day included leaders in the Kenyan government, and representatives of churches, mission organizations and non-governmental organizations. The meeting received wide publicity. It was evident that creation care is neither a selfish interest of the developed North, nor a minority enthusiasm peculiar to bird-watchers or flower-lovers, but an increasingly mainline Christian concern.

When I first read *An Evangelical Declaration on the Care of Creation*, although on some points I might have wished to express myself a little differently, I nevertheless found myself in full agreement with its basis and thrust. I gladly endorsed it, and now welcome this substantial commentary on it.

Christians have been slow to respond to the imperatives of creation care, and we evangelical believers in particular have been even more laggardly. In the following pages, some reasons for this slowness are examined, calling for repentance, and a solid biblical foundation is established, calling for action.

Scripture tells us that 'the earth is the LORD's' (Ps. 24:1) and also that 'the earth he has given to man' (Ps. 115:16). These assertions complement rather than contradict each other. The Earth belongs to God by creation and to us by delegation. This does not mean that he has handed it over to us in such a way as to relinquish his own rights over it, but rather that he has given us the responsibility to preserve and develop the Earth on his behalf.

How, then, should we relate to the Earth? If we remember its creation by God and its delegation to us, we will avoid two opposite extremes and instead develop a third and better relationship to nature.

First, we will avoid the *deification* of nature. This is the mistake of pantheists, who identify the Creator with his creation, of animists, who populate the natural world with spirits, and of the New Age's Gaia movement, which attributes to nature its own self-contained, self-regulating and self-perpetuating mechanisms. But all such confusions are derogatory to the Creator. The Christian desacralizing of nature (the recognition that it is creation, not Creator) was an indispensable prelude to the whole scientific enterprise and is essential to the development of the Earth's resources today. We *respect* nature because God made it; we do not *reverence* nature as if it were God and inviolable.

Secondly, we must avoid the opposite extreme, which is the *exploitation* of nature. We must not treat nature obsequiously as if it were God, nor behave towards it arrogantly as if we were God. Genesis 1 has been unjustly blamed for environmental irresponsibility. It is true that God commissioned the human race to 'have dominion over' the earth and to 'subdue' it (Gen. 1:26–28, NRSV), and these two Hebrew verbs are forceful. It would be absurd, however, to imagine that he who *created* the Earth then handed it over to us to be *destroyed*. No, the *dominion* God has given us is a responsible stewardship, not a destructive domination.

The third and correct relationship between human beings and nature is that of *cooperation* with God. To be sure, we are ourselves a part of creation, just as dependent on the Creator as are all his creatures. Yet at the same time he has deliberately humbled himself to make a divine–human partnership necessary. He created the Earth, but then told us to subdue it. He planted the garden, but then put Adam in it 'to work it and take care of it' (Gen. 2:15). This is often called the *cultural* mandate. For what God has given us is *nature*, whereas what we do with it is *culture*. We are not only to conserve the environment, but also to develop its resources for the common good.

It is a noble calling to cooperate with God for the fulfilment of his purposes, to transform the created order for the pleasure and profit of all.

In this way our work is to be an expression of our worship, since our care of the creation will reflect our love for the Creator.

A final thought: it is possible to overstate this emphasis on human work in the conservation and transformation of the environment. In his excellent exposition of the first three chapters of Genesis, *In the Beginning* (1984), Henri Blocher argues that the climax of Genesis 1 is not the creation of man the worker but the institution of the Sabbath for man the worshipper; it is not our toil (subduing the Earth) but the laying aside of our toil on the Sabbath day. For the Sabbath relativizes the importance of work. It protects us from a total absorption in our work as if it were to be the be-all and end-all of our existence. It is not. We human beings find our humanness not only in relation to the Earth, which we are to transform, but in relation to God, whom we are to worship; not only in relation to the creation, but especially in relation to the Creator. God intends our work to be an expression of our worship, and our care of the creation to reflect our love for the Creator. Only then, whatever we do, in word or deed, shall we be able to do it to the glory of God (1 Cor. 10:31).

These and other biblical themes are opened up in both the *Declaration* and the commentary on it. They deserve our careful study.

JOHN STOTT
December 1999

Part I
Rationale

This book will have failed if it is regarded as merely 'another' book on the environment from a group of 'green' Christians, however dedicated and informed. It is both less and more than that. It is less because it is specifically and mainly a theological commentary on a particular document (*An Evangelical Declaration on the Care of Creation*); it is more because this is not simply an exercise in advocacy: the commentators are united in their Bible-based understanding of the environment as God's creation entrusted to our care and wonder. This unity is particularly compelling because those who have contributed to this volume are not a homogeneity of committed econuts, but mainstream theologians and others with a robust concern for truth, wherever it may lead.

The Care of Creation arises from three truisms:

1. A virtually unanimous and sombre acknowledgment that humans have damaged their environment. The UK Government's submission to the Earth Summit (the United Nations Conference on Environment and Development, UNCED) in Rio de Janeiro in 1992 stated:

> Ever since the Age of Enlightenment, we have had an almost boundless faith in our own intelligence and in the benign consequences of our actions. Whatever the discoveries of science, whatever the rate at which we multiplied as a species, whatever the rate at which we destroyed other species, whatever the changes we

made to our seas and landscape, we have believed that the world would stay much the same in all its fundamentals. We now know that this is no longer true. This perception could have consequences for national action and international diplomacy as far-reaching as those which resulted from the splitting of the atom ... Increasingly we understand that the ways we multiply, produce energy, use natural resources and produce waste threaten to change fundamentally the balance of our global environment. We may not be seeing the end of Nature, but Nature is certainly under threat (*This Common Inheritance*, 1990: 9).

2. A general feeling of helplessness on the part of individuals. What can *I* do about climate change, species extinction, genetic holocaust, and so on? There is certainly an increased environmental awareness nowadays, marked by an unease about waste and by gestures towards recycling. Worthy though these are, they seem either futile or even pharisaical when faced with major disasters like Bhopal, Chernobyl, BSE or the ozone hole. The current angst is deeper and strikes at our very humanness. Robin Grove-White (1992: 28) has suggested that

Rather than the environmental agenda being presented to us from on high by science, the actual selection of issues constituting the agenda becomes seen as constructed socially, as a political response to pressures from 'below' – pressures which in turn arise from human beings responding gropingly to a sense of the ways in which their moral, social and physical identities are being threatened and misrepresented in ways they do not fully understand.

This book is not a DIY manual for concerned environmentalists, nor is it a set of prescriptions for dealing with specific problems (climate change, biodiversity loss, pollution, genetic engineering and so on). Rather, it is an examination and commentary on the underlying issues which have to be dealt with before we can robustly and sustainably produce answers to applied questions.

3. Christians dither – caught between a Scylla of welcoming environmental disasters as a sign of the 'end-times' and a Charybdis of shipwreck on pantheism and New Age nightmares. This is not to ignore

valiant cries from both individuals and church assemblies,[1] but there has not been – nor is there – any general agreement about Christian commitment on priorities or actions about creation care. If environmental problems are as serious as the experts make out, Christians clearly have a need to focus their response as a matter of both survival and significant apologetics. But there is a deeper issue: if creation care is a divine mandate laid on all humankind, and if Christ's saving work really did involve reconciling to the Father '*all* things, whether things on earth or things in heaven' (Col. 1:20), then neglecting creation care is a sin and not merely an option in an overcrowded agenda.

An Evangelical Declaration on the Care of Creation arose out of the frustration of some of those who attended the culmination of the World Council of Churches series of consultations on the 'Justice, Peace and the Integrity of Creation' (see below, p. 28) at Seoul, Korea, in March 1990 (Sider 1990; Sugden 1990). Faced with the legitimate complaint that the command to the human race to 'fill the earth and subdue it, have dominion over [it]' (Gen. 1:28, REB) had led to a gross exploitation of creation, the Seoul Assembly decided that the way forward was to dethrone humanity from its unique role as 'the image of God' (Sugden 1993). This prompted a meeting in August 1992 of the Theological Commission of the World Evangelical Fellowship and the Au Sable Forum at the Au Sable Institute, Michigan,[2] whose report 'Evangelical Christianity and the Environment'[3] stimulated the formation of an Evangelical Environmental Network (EEN).[4] The *Declaration* was launched in 1994 as one of the first products of the EEN (p. 190).

The EEN sought (and received) endorsement of the *Declaration* by several hundred church leaders throughout the world. Not surprisingly, some of these commented on particular aspects of the document. As a result it has seemed both sensible and useful to solicit specific commendations or criticisms on the *Declaration* and the implications. The suggestion for this commentary came from Professor Oliver O'Donovan of Oxford University (see below, pp. 90–93); its maturation is a sign that the message of the *Declaration* could be helped by scholarly examination and exposition. I was responsible for encouraging British Christians to support the *Declaration*. I hope this volume will stimulate and facilitate its understanding and application on both sides of the Atlantic (which should be interpreted to mean in both Eastern and Western hemispheres, both north and south of the Equator; in other words, throughout the world).

My thanks are due to all those who have contributed to this volume. The comments of Calvin DeWitt (pp. 60–73) formed part of the biblical input to the drafters of the *Declaration* and have appeared previously (DeWitt 1993). Lynn White's paper (pp. 31–42) first appeared in *Science* in 1967. Ron Sider's article (pp. 43–49) is a development of one published in *Christianity Today* (1993). I am grateful to all who have written for this volume. They have all agreed to forgo any payment for their efforts, and any proceeds from sales will go to The John Ray Initiative (pp. 184–185). And, finally, thanks are due to Bishop Timothy Dudley-Smith, who has written a hymn specially to celebrate creation care. This is printed on pp. 205–206.

An Evangelical Declaration on the Care of Creation

The *Declaration* was formally issued in 1994 to assert and emphasize that this Earth belongs to God and that we are responsible to him for it. This belief underlines the historical Christian doctrine that we are stewards of creation, responsible to the Creator for our treatment of the environment (Attfield 1991). The *Declaration* reaffirms this understanding in its call to insist and encourage the church to maintain the biblical mandate for creation care in the face of claims that Christianity is irrelevant or incompetent to react significantly and positively to environmental assaults. The *Declaration* has been endorsed by church leaders on both sides of the Atlantic.

The *Declaration* sets out five Christian affirmations relevant to discernible violations of creation, identifies four spiritual responses, and then calls upon all Christians to seek to apply these responses in specified ways.

The full text of the *Declaration* is as follows.

An Evangelical Declaration on the Care of Creation

The earth is the LORD's, and the fullness thereof. (Psalm 24:1)

As followers of Jesus Christ, committed to the full authority of the Scriptures, and aware of the ways we have degraded creation, we believe that biblical faith is essential to the solution of our ecological problems.

- Because we worship and honour the Creator, we seek to cherish and care for the creation.
- Because we have sinned, we have failed in our stewardship of creation. Therefore we repent of the way we have polluted, distorted, or destroyed so much of the Creator's work.
- Because, in Christ, God has healed our alienation from God and extended to us the first fruits of the reconciliation of all things, we commit ourselves to working in the power of the Holy Spirit to share the Good News of Christ in word and deed, to work for the reconciliation of all people in Christ, and to extend Christ's healing to suffering creation.
- Because we await the time when even the groaning creation will be restored to wholeness, we commit ourselves to work vigorously to protect and heal that creation for the honour and glory of the Creator – whom we know dimly through creation, but meet fully through Scripture and in Christ.

We and our children face a growing crisis in the health of the creation in which we are embedded, and through which, by God's grace, we are sustained. Yet we continue to degrade that creation.

- These degradations of creation can be summed up as: 1) land degradation; 2) deforestation; 3) species extinction; 4) water degradation; 5) global toxification; 6) the alteration of atmosphere; 7) human and cultural degradation.
- Many of these degradations are signs that we are pressing against the finite limits God has set for creation. With continued population growth, these degradations will become more severe. Our responsibility is not only to bear and nurture children, but to nurture their home on earth. We respect the institution of marriage as the way God has given to ensure thoughtful procreation of children and their nurture to the glory of God.

• We recognize that human poverty is both a cause and a consequence of environmental degradation.

Many concerned people, convinced that environmental problems are more spiritual than technological, are exploring the world's ideologies and religions in search of non-Christian spiritual resources for the healing of the earth. As followers of Jesus Christ, we believe that the Bible calls us to respond in four ways:

• First, God calls us to confess and repent of attitudes which devalue creation, and which twist or ignore biblical revelation to support our misuse of it. Forgetting that 'the earth is the Lord's', we have often simply used creation and forgotten our responsibility to care for it.

• Second, our actions and attitudes towards the earth need to proceed from the centre of our faith, and be rooted in the fullness of God's revelation in Christ and the Scriptures. We resist both ideologies which would presume the Gospel has nothing to do with the care of non-human creation and also ideologies which would reduce the Gospel to nothing more than the care of that creation.

• Third, we seek carefully to learn all that the Bible tells us about the Creator, creation, and the human task. In our life and words we declare that full good news for all creation which is still waiting 'with eager longing for the revealing of the children of God' (Rom. 8:19).

• Fourth, we seek to understand what creation reveals about God's divinity, sustaining presence, and everlasting power, and what creation teaches us of its God-given order and the principles by which it works.

Thus we call on all those who are committed to the truth of the Gospel of Jesus Christ to affirm the following principles of biblical faith, and to seek ways of living out these principles in our personal lives, our churches, and society.

• The cosmos, in all its beauty, wildness, and life-giving bounty, is the work of our personal and loving Creator.

• Our creating God is prior to and other than creation, yet intimately involved with it, upholding each thing in its freedom, and all things in relationships of intricate complexity. God is *transcendent*, while lovingly sustaining each creature; and *immanent*, while wholly other than creation and not to be confused with it.

• God the Creator is relational in very nature, revealed as three persons in One. Likewise, the creation which God intended is a symphony of individual creatures in harmonious relationship.

• The Creator's concern is for all creatures. God declares all creation 'good' (Gen. 1:31); promises care in a covenant with all creatures (Gen. 9:9–17); delights in creatures which have no human apparent usefulness (Job 39 – 41); and wills, in Christ, 'to reconcile all things to himself' (Col. 1:20).

• Men, women, and children, have a unique responsibility to the Creator; at the same time we are *creatures*, shaped by the same processes and embedded in the same systems of physical, chemical, and biological interconnections which sustain other creatures.

• Men, women, and children, created in God's image, also have a unique responsibility for creation. Our actions should both sustain creation's fruitfulness and preserve creation's powerful testimony to its Creator.

• Our God-given, stewardly talents have often been warped from their intended purpose: that we know, name, keep and delight in God's creatures; that we nourish civilization in love, creativity and obedience to God; and that we offer creation and civilization back in praise to the Creator. We have ignored our creaturely limits and have used the earth with greed, rather than care.

• The earthly result of human sin has been a perverted stewardship, a patchwork of garden and wasteland in which the waste is increasing. 'There is no faithfulness, no love, no acknowledgment of God in the land ... Because of this the land mourns, and all who live in it waste away' (Hosea 4:1, 3). Thus, one consequence of our misuse of the earth is an unjust denial of God's created bounty to other human beings, both now and in the future.

• God's purpose in Christ is to heal and bring to wholeness not only persons but the entire created order. 'For God was pleased to have all his fullness dwell in him, and through him to reconcile to himself all things, whether things on earth or things in heaven, by making peace through his blood shed on the cross' (Col. 1:19–20).

• In Jesus Christ, believers are forgiven, transformed and brought into God's kingdom. 'If anyone is in Christ, there is a new creation' (2 Cor. 5:17). The presence of the kingdom of God is marked not only by renewed fellowship with God, but also by renewed harmony and justice between people, and by renewed harmony and justice between people and the rest of the created world. 'You will go out with joy and be led forth in peace; the mountains and the hills will burst into song before you, and all the trees of the field will clap their hands' (Isa. 55:12).

We believe that in Christ there is hope, not only for men, women and children, but also for the rest of creation which is suffering from the consequences of human sin.

• Therefore we call upon all Christians to reaffirm that all creation is God's; that God created it good; and that God is renewing it in Christ.

• We encourage deeper reflection on the substantial biblical and theological teaching which speaks of God's work of redemption in terms of the renewal and completion of God's purpose in creation.

• We seek a deeper reflection on the wonders of God's creation and the principles by which creation works. We also urge a careful consideration of how our corporate and individual actions respect and comply with God's ordinances for creation.

• We encourage Christians to incorporate the extravagant creativity of God into their lives by increasing the nurturing role of beauty and the arts in their personal, ecclesiastical, and social patterns.

• We urge individual Christians and churches to be centres of creation's care and renewal, both delighting in creation as God's gift, and enjoying it as God's provision, in ways which sustain and heal the damaged fabric of the creation which God has entrusted to us.

• We recall Jesus' words that our lives do not consist in the abundance of our possessions, and therefore we urge followers of Jesus to resist the allure of wastefulness and overconsumption by making personal lifestyle choices that express humility, forbearance, self-restraint and frugality.

• We call on Christians to work for godly, just, and sustainable economies which reflect God's sovereign economy and enable men, women and children to flourish along with all the diversity of creation. We recognize that poverty forces people to degrade creation in order to survive; therefore we support the development of just, free economies which empower the poor and create abundance without diminishing creation's bounty.

• We commit ourselves to work for responsible public policies which embody the principles of biblical stewardship of creation.

• We invite Christians – individuals, congregations and organizations – to join with us in this evangelical declaration on the environment, becoming a covenant people in an ever-widening circle of biblical care for creation.

• We call upon Christians to listen to and work with all those who are concerned about the healing of creation, with an eagerness both to learn from them and also to share with them our conviction that the God whom all people sense in creation (Acts 17:27) is known fully only in the Word made flesh in Christ the living God, who made and sustains all things.

• We make this declaration knowing that until Christ returns to reconcile all things, we are called to be faithful stewards of God's good garden, our earthly home.

Part II
Context

It should not be necessary for Christians or Jews or, for that matter, Muslims specifically to affirm that God is sovereign in his creation. Yet the apparent clarity of scriptural teaching (that the Earth is the Lord's by creation and redemption, that Christ has reconciled all things to the Father and all things 'hold together' in him, and that God has entrusted his 'good creation' to us as his vice-gerents) has repeatedly been clouded by centuries of debate and confusing emphases.

In his attack on Gnosticism, Irenaeus (AD 130–200) underlined the cosmic significance of the incarnation, death and resurrection of Jesus Christ as set out in the Pauline and Johannine writings, and he developed a theology of nature wholly different from that implied by the Christian Gnosticism of his time (reviewed by Glacken 1967; Santmire 1985). This tradition never developed properly because of resurgent (Neo)Platonism, which muddied interpretations by insisting on an intrinsic invariableness in the world so that change was seen as theologically impossible. Others have written about the difficulties that this imposed on the development of science (e.g. Mayr 1982; McGrath 1998). From the point of view of a mature Christian attitude to the environment, it meant that for a long time there was an assumption that the *status quo* was natural and God-given; human management was implicitly assumed to be properly concerned with preservation rather than management. Notwithstanding, a Christian understanding of stewardship was clearly expressed in Benedictine practices which date back to the sixth century (Black 1970; Attfield 1991).

25

As Bauckham (p. 99 below) points out, this was different from its modern guise, but the claim that Christian stewardship dates only from the late seventeenth century[1] is too simple.

As far as modern attitudes are concerned, the importance laid on personal salvation by the Reformers reinforced the scholastic Platonism of the Middle Ages and encouraged the separation of the early modern science from mainstream Christian faith. This did not affect the religious commitments of, for example, the founders of the Royal Society in 1660, who were overtly Christian in their beliefs, but it meant that the non-human creation tended to be regarded as a mere stage for God's saving works.

In a highly influential paper (reprinted below on pp. 31–42), Lynn White (1967) argued that Christianity had 'de-sacralized' nature, and allowed it to be exploited without restraint. He wrote that 'we are superior to nature, contemptuous of it, willing to use it for our slightest whim'. He quoted Ronald Reagan as saying, 'when you've seen one redwood tree, you've seen them all'. White's interpretation has been challenged on both historical and theological grounds (e.g. Sheldon 1989; Whitney 1993; see also McGrath's essay, pp. 86–89), but his article has been reprinted in many places and still exercises a considerable influence. For example, Francis Schaeffer (1970) included its text in his pioneering *Pollution and the Death of Man*, describing it as 'a brilliant article ... I believe he is completely right. Men do what they think. Whatever their world view is, this is the thing which will spill over into the external world' (1970: 10). Schaeffer accepted White's thesis enthusiastically; it fitted in with his own view of human alienation from God's purposes: 'A truly biblical Christianity has a real answer to the ecological crisis. It offers a balanced and healthy attitude to nature, arising from the truth of its creation by God; it offers the hope here and now of substantial healing in nature of some of the results of the Fall, arising from the truth of redemption in Christ' (1970: 58).

A number of non-Christian writers have echoed White's accusation. For example, the distinguished landscape architect Ian McHarg (1969) trumpeted,

If one seeks licence for those who would increase radioactivity, create canals and harbours with atomic bombs, employ poisons without constraint, or give consent to the bulldozer mentality, there could be no better injunction than the text, 'God blessed them (the newly formed human beings), and said to them, Be fruitful and increase, fill the earth and subdue it, have dominion over the fish in the sea, the birds of the air, and everything that moves on the earth' (Genesis 1:28) ... Dominion and subjugation must be expunged as the biblical injunction of man's relation to nature (1969: 197).

Pioneer conservationist Max Nicholson (1970) has argued similarly: 'The first step [for responsible environmental care] must be plainly to reject and to scrub out the complacent image of Man the Conqueror of Nature, and of Man Licensed by God to conduct himself as the earth's worst pest' (1970: 264).

There are undoubtedly many Christians who have regarded the Genesis command to dominion and subjugation as a mandate for plundering the environment for all that they can take, but it is their interpretation of the Bible that is at fault, not the command itself. It is important to note that

1. God's command in Genesis was in the context of human beings created 'in his image', which involves trustworthiness and responsibility (Moule 1964).

2. Hebrew rule was meant to be a servant kingship, exemplified by the instructions given to David and Solomon, and ideally shown by Jesus Christ; it was not a despotic potency.

Sheldon (1992) summarizes a large volume of literature which examines White's arguments: 'The consensus is that White's and McHarg's scriptural analysis is deficient and thus their conclusion faulty. They based their case primarily on the single passage in Genesis dealing with dominion and failed to consider the numerous other scriptural teachings on the concern, love and care for the Creation' (1992: 26). But White's influence still persists. Max Oelschlaeger (1994) begins his book *Caring for Creation* with a confession:

For most of my adult life I believed, as many environmentalists do, that religion was the primary cause of ecological crisis ... I was a true believer: if only people would listen to the ecologists, economists, and others who made claims that they could 'manage planet Earth', we would all be saved. I lost that faith by bits and pieces, especially through the demystification of two ecological problems – climate heating and extinction of species – and by discovering the roots of my prejudice against religion. *That bias had*

> *grown out of my reading of Lynn White's famous essay ...* (1994: 1–2;
> my italics).

In other words, Oelschlaeger, like Luther centuries before him, was convinced by looking hard at real phenomena as distinct from received authority.

The misrepresentation of the Christian faith as uncaring of creation has probably played a part in diverting people towards other belief systems – Eastern religions supposedly 'kind' towards nature, New Age in its various manifestations, Matthew Fox's creation spirituality, and other faiths or variations. All of them have in common a degree of pantheism: in seeking to respect the environment, men and women devise ways of worshipping the creation in various ways or to extents; the biblical distinction between Creator and creation becomes blurred in the name of 'resacralizing' creation.

This tendency has been aggravated by the debates over evolution and creationism in some parts of Christendom; these have distracted attention away from creation care, particularly in conservative circles (Berry 1995). There have, of course, been strong statements of creation doctrine from both Christian bodies (e.g. an Archbishops' Commission of the Church of England: Montefiore 1975) and concerned individuals (e.g. Montefiore 1969; Cobb 1972). However, the biggest initiative has undoubtedly been the Justice, Peace and the Integrity of Creation Programme (JPIC) of the World Council of Churches (Gosling 1992; Niles 1992).

JPIC was formally inaugurated at the sixth assembly of the World Council of Churches in Vancouver in 1983, when the Council, urged in particular by Jürgen Moltmann (see below, pp. 107–113) and responding to prompting from the World Alliance of Reformed Churches, added the need for maintaining the 'integrity of creation' to its long-established programme of pursuing 'peace with justice'. This was developed through a 'conciliar' process from local to regional assemblies, and finally to a world convocation in Seoul in 1990 (see above, p. 28 and also the article by Ron Sider, pp. 43–49). As already noted, this provoked a meeting of evangelicals at the Au Sable Institute in 1992, and thence to the setting up of an Evangelical Environmental Network and drafting of the *Declaration*.

The JPIC process did not take place in a vacuum. In 1986, the Worldwide Fund for Nature (WWF) held its twenty-fifth anniversary meeting in Assisi, Italy, and issued a set of *Assisi Declarations* (1986) containing 'messages on man and nature from Buddhism, Christianity, Hinduism, Islam and Judaism' (Baha'i was added the next year). This led to WWF setting up a Network of Conservation and Religion. An expansion of the Christian position was subsequently produced after a series of consultations at St George's House, Windsor Castle (Edinburgh and Mann 1989).

This convergence continued with the publication in January 1990 of an 'Open Letter to the Religious Community' and, in 1992, 1,575 scientists co-ordinated by Henry Kendall, Nobel Laureate and Chairman of the Union of Concerned Scientists, signed 'The World's Scientists' Warning to Humanity' (reproduced by Ehrlich and Ehrlich 1996). Also in 1992, the National Science Academies of the US and Britain issued their first-ever joint statement, on 'Population growth, resource consumption and a sustainable world'. There followed in 1993 a document signed by representatives of fifty-eight of the world's scientific academies, agreeing that a 'common goal is improving the quality of life for all people, those living today and succeeding generations, ensuring their social economic, and personal well-being with guarantees of fundamental human rights, and allowing them to live harmoniously with a protected environment'.

Meanwhile, the Earth Summit (the United Nations Conference on Environment and Development, UNCED) was held in Rio in 1991. There was a non-governmental conference associated with the main conference, and Christians were represented at this. Several books were published (e.g. Campolo 1992; Seaton 1992) and events organized to build on the environmental interest created by UNCED, but these attracted only local attention. The Earth Summit proper led to agreement on Framework Conventions on Climate Change, and on Biodiversity, on a research programme for the twenty-first century (Agenda 21), and on a set of principles described as the Rio Declaration. Although subsequent action has been less than many hoped, the conference was successful in provoking recognition by developing countries that they share a common environment with the developed countries. Over the decades leading to Rio, there had been bitter arguments between 'North' and 'South', with the latter accusing the industrial nations of treating the environment as an excuse to restrict development. Such debates continue, but are now marked by a greater realization of the common and finite world which is shared by all.

A significant Christian recognition of the environment was made by the

Anglican Consultative Council in 1990 (*Mission in a Broken World*). This body reaffirmed what it called

> a consistent view of mission ... defined in a four-fold way ...
>
> a. to proclaim the good news of the Kingdom;
> b. to teach, baptize and nurture new believers;
> c. to respond to human need by loving service;
> d. to seek to transform the unjust structures of society.

It then added a fifth mark:

> e. to strive to safeguard the integrity of creation and sustain and renew the life of the earth.

The justification for this was that it 'acknowledges the concern and apologetic relevance of Creation care for the Church's ministry and evangelism'.

This is the world we find ourselves in at the turn of the Millennium. For the Christian it is God's world and we labour to tend the garden with all men and women whatever their religion. But it is also the world (not only the human race) for which Christ died, and we have a responsibility to share this news with all our neighbours. This is the context in which we have a *Declaration on the Care of Creation* to focus our thoughts and actions.

1

The historical roots of our ecologic crisis[1]

Lynn White, Jr

Lynn White, Jr, was Professor of History at the University of California, Los Angeles, when he gave the lecture reprinted here, at a meeting of the American Association for the Advancement of Science in 1966.

A conversation with Aldous Huxley not infrequently put one at the receiving end of an unforgettable monologue. About a year before his lamented death he was discoursing on a favourite topic: man's unnatural treatment of nature and its sad results. To illustrate his point he told how, during the previous summer, he had returned to a little valley in England where he had spent many happy months as a child. Once it had been composed of delightful grassy glades; now it was becoming overgrown with unsightly brush because the rabbits that formerly kept such growth under control had largely succumbed to a disease, myxomatosis, that was deliberately introduced by the local farmers to reduce the rabbits' destruction of crops. Being something of a Philistine, I could be silent no longer, even in the interest of great rhetoric. I interrupted to point out that the rabbit itself had been brought as a domestic animal to England in 1176, presumably to improve the protein diet of the peasantry.

All forms of life modify their contexts. The most spectacular and benign instance is doubtless the coral polyp. By serving its own ends, it has created a vast undersea world favourable to thousands of other kinds of animals and plants. Ever since man became a numerous species he has affected his environment notably. The hypothesis that his fire-drive method of hunting created the world's great grasslands and helped to exterminate the monster

31

mammals of the Pleistocene from much of the globe is plausible, if not proved. For six millennia at least, the banks of the lower Nile have been a human artefact rather than the swampy African jungle which nature, apart from man, would have made it. The Aswan Dam, flooding 5,000 square miles, is only the latest stage in a long process. In many regions terracing or irrigation, overgrazing, the cutting of forests by Romans to build ships to fight Carthaginians or by Crusaders to solve the logistics problems of their expeditions, have profoundly changed some ecologies. Observation that the French landscape falls into two basic types, the open fields of the north and the *bocage* of the south and west, inspired Marc Bloch to undertake his classic study of medieval agricultural methods. Quite unintentionally, changes in human ways often affect non-human nature. It has been noted, for example, that the advent of the automobile eliminated huge flocks of sparrows that once fed on the horse manure littering every street.

The history of ecologic change is still so rudimentary that we know little about what really happened, or what the results were. The extinction of the European aurochs as late as 1627 would seem to have been a simple case of overenthusiastic hunting. On more intricate matters it often is impossible to find solid information. For a thousand years or more the Frisians and Hollanders have been pushing back the North Sea, and the process is culminating in our own time in the reclamation of the Zuider Zee. What, if any, species of animals, birds, fish, shore life, or plants have died out in the process? In their epic combat with Neptune, have the Netherlanders overlooked ecological values in such a way that the quality of human life in the Netherlands has suffered? I cannot discover that the questions have ever been asked, much less answered.

People, then, have often been a dynamic element in their own environment, but in the present state of historical scholarship we usually do not know exactly when, where, or with what effects man-induced changes came. As we enter the last third of the twentieth century, however, concern for the problem of ecologic backlash is mounting feverishly. Natural science, conceived as the effort to understand the nature of things, had flourished in several eras and among several peoples. Similarly there had been an age-old accumulation of technological skills, sometimes growing rapidly, sometimes slowly. But it was not until about four generations ago that Western Europe and North America arranged a marriage between science and technology, a union of the theoretical and the empirical approaches to our natural environment. The emergence in widespread practice of the Baconian creed that scientific knowledge means technological power over nature can scarcely be dated before about 1850, save in the chemical industries, where it is anticipated in the eighteenth century. Its acceptance as a normal pattern of action may mark the greatest event in human history since the invention of agriculture, and perhaps in non-human terrestrial history as well.

Almost at once the new situation forced the crystallization of the novel concept of ecology; indeed, the word *ecology* first appeared in the English language in 1873. Today, less than a century later, the impact of our race upon the environment has so increased in force that it has changed in essence. When the first cannons were fired, in the early fourteenth century, they affected ecology by sending workers scrambling to the forests and mountains for more potash, sulphur, iron ore, and charcoal, with some resulting erosion and deforestation. Hydrogen bombs are of a different order: a war fought with them might alter the genetics of all life on this planet. By 1285 London had a smog problem arising from the burning of soft coal, but our present combustion of fossil fuels threatens to change the chemistry of the globe's atmosphere as a whole, with consequences which we are only beginning to guess. With the population explosion, the carcinoma of planless urbanism, the now geological deposits of sewage and garbage, surely no creature other than man has ever managed to foul its nest in such short order.

There are many calls to action, but specific proposals, however worthy as individual items, seem too partial, palliative, negative: ban the bomb, tear down the billboards, give the Hindus contraceptives and tell them to eat their sacred cows. The simplest solution to any suspect change is, of course, to stop it, or, better yet, to revert to a romanticized past: make those ugly petrol stations look like Anne Hathaway's cottage or (in the Far West) like ghost-town saloons. The 'wilderness area' mentality invariably advocates deep-freezing an ecology, whether San Gimignano or the High Sierra, as it was before the first Kleenex was dropped. But neither atavism nor prettification will cope with the ecologic crisis of our time.

What shall we do? No one yet knows. Unless we think about fundamentals, our specific measures may produce new backlashes more serious than those they are designed to remedy.

As a beginning we should try to clarify our thinking by looking, in some historical depth, at the presuppositions that underlie modern technology and science. Science was traditionally aristocratic, speculative, intellectual in intent; technology was lower-class, empirical, action-oriented. The quite sudden fusion of these two, towards the middle of the nineteenth century, is surely related to the slightly prior and contemporary democratic revolutions which, by reducing social barriers, tended to assert a functional unity of brain and hand. Our ecologic crisis is the product of an emerging, entirely novel, democratic culture. The issue is whether a democratized world can survive its own implications. Presumably we cannot unless we rethink our axioms.

The Western traditions of technology and science

One thing is so certain that it seems stupid to verbalize it: both modern technology and modern science are distinctively Occidental. Our technology has absorbed elements from all over the world, notably from China; yet everywhere today, whether in Japan or in Nigeria, successful technology is Western. Our science is the heir to all the sciences of the past, especially perhaps to the work of the great Islamic scientists of the Middle Ages, who so often outdid the ancient Greeks in skill and perspicacity: al-Razi in medicine, for example; or ibn-al-Haytham in optics; or Omar Khayyám in mathematics. Indeed, not a few works of such geniuses seem to have vanished in the original Arabic and to survive only in medieval Latin translations that helped to lay the foundations for later Western developments. Today, around the globe, all significant science is Western in style and method, whatever the pigmentation or language of the scientists.

A second pair of facts is less well recognized because they result from quite recent historical scholarship. The leadership of the West, both in technology and in science, is far older than the so-called Scientific Revolution of the seventeenth century or the so-called Industrial Revolution of the eighteenth century. These terms are in fact outmoded and obscure the true nature of what they try to describe – significant stages in two long and separate developments. By AD 1000 at the latest – and perhaps, feebly, as much as 200 years earlier – the West began to apply water power to industrial processes other than milling grain. This was followed in the late twelfth century by the harnessing of wind power. From simple beginnings, but with remarkable consistency of style, the West rapidly expanded its skills in the development of power machinery, labour-saving devices, and automation. Those who doubt should contemplate that most monumental achievement in the history of automation: the weight-driven mechanical clock, which appeared in two forms in the early fourteenth century. Not in craftsmanship but in basic technological capacity, the Latin West of the later Middle Ages far outstripped its elaborate, sophisticated, and aesthetically magnificent sister cultures, Byzantium and Islam. In 1444 a great Greek ecclesiastic, Bessarion, who had gone to Italy, wrote a letter to a prince in Greece. He is amazed by the superiority of Western ships, arms, textiles, glass. But above all he is astonished by the spectacle of waterwheels sawing timbers and pumping the bellows of blast furnaces. Clearly, he had seen nothing of the sort in the Near East.

By the end of the fifteenth century the technological superiority of Europe was such that its small, mutually hostile nations could spill out over all the rest of the world, conquering, looting, and colonizing. The symbol of this technological superiority is the fact that Portugal, one of the weakest states of the Occident, was able to become, and to remain for a century, mistress of the East Indies. And we must remember that the technology of Vasco da Gama and Albuquerque was built by pure empiricism, drawing remarkably little support or inspiration from science.

In the present-day vernacular understanding, modern science is supposed to have begun in 1543, when both Copernicus and Vesalius published their great works. It is not derogation of their accomplishments, however, to point out that such structures as the *Fabrica* and the *De revolutionibus* do not appear overnight. The distinctive Western tradition of science, in fact, began in the late eleventh century with a massive movement of translation of Arabic and Greek scientific works into Latin. A few notable books – Theophrastus, for example – escaped the West's avid new appetite for science, but within less than 200 years effectively the entire corpus of Greek and Muslim science was available in Latin, and was being eagerly read and criticized in the new European universities. Out of criticism arose new observation, speculation, and increasing distrust of ancient authorities. By the late thirteenth century Europe had seized global scientific leadership from the faltering hands of Islam. It would be as absurd to deny the profound originality of Newton, Galileo, or Copernicus as to deny that of the fourteenth century scholastic scientists like Buridan or Oresme on whose work they built. Before the eleventh century, science scarcely existed in the Latin West, even in Roman times. From the eleventh century onward, the scientific sector of Occidental culture has increased in a steady crescendo.

Since both our technological and our scientific movements got their start, acquired their character, and achieved world dominance in the Middle Ages, it would seem that we cannot understand their nature or their present impact upon ecology without examining fundamental medieval assumptions and developments.

Medieval view of man and nature

Until recently, agriculture has been the chief occupation even in 'advanced' societies; hence, any change in methods of tillage has much importance. Early ploughs, drawn by two oxen, did not normally turn the sod but merely scratched it. Thus, cross-ploughing was needed and fields tended to be squarish. In the fairly light soils and semi-arid climates of the Near East and Mediterranean, this worked well. But such a plough was inappropriate to the wet climate and often sticky soils of northern Europe. By the latter part of the seventh century after Christ, however, following obscure beginnings, certain northern peasants were using an entirely new kind of plough, equipped with a vertical knife to cut the line of the furrow, a horizontal share to slice under the sod, and a mouldboard to turn it over. The friction of this plough with the soil was so great that it normally required not two but eight oxen. It attacked the land with such violence that cross-ploughing was not needed, and fields tended to be shaped in long strips.

In the days of the scratch-plough, fields were distributed generally in units capable of supporting a single family. Subsistence farming was the presupposition. But no peasant owned eight oxen: to use the new and more efficient plough, peasants pooled their oxen to form large plough-teams, originally receiving (it would appear) ploughed strips in proportion to their contribution. Thus, distribution of land was based no longer on the needs of a family but, rather, on the capacity of a power machine to till the earth. Man's relation to the soil was profoundly changed. Formerly man had been part of nature; now he was the exploiter of nature. Nowhere else in the world did farmers develop any analogous agricultural implement. Is it coincidence that modern technology, with its ruthlessness toward nature, has so largely been produced by descendants of these peasants of northern Europe?

This same exploitive attitude appears slightly before AD 830 in Western illustrated calendars. In older calendars the months were shown as passive personifications. The new Frankish calendars, which set the style for the Middle Ages, are very different: they show men coercing the world around them – ploughing, harvesting, chopping trees, butchering pigs. Man and nature are two things, and man is master.

These novelties seem to be in harmony with larger intellectual patterns. What people do about their ecology depends on what they think about themselves in relation to things around them. Human ecology is deeply conditioned by beliefs about our nature and destiny – that is, by religion. To Western eyes this is very evident in, say, India or Ceylon. It is equally true of ourselves and of our medieval ancestors.

The victory of Christianity over paganism was the greatest psychic revolution in the history of our culture. It has become fashionable today to say that, for better or worse, we live in 'the post-Christian age'. Certainly the forms of our thinking and language have largely ceased to be Christian, but to my eye the substance often remains amazingly akin to that of the past. Our daily habits of action, for example, are dominated by an implicit faith in perpetual progress which was unknown either to Greco-Roman antiquity or to the Orient. It is rooted in, and is indefensible apart from, Judeo-Christian teleology. The fact that Communists share it merely helps to show what can be demonstrated on many other grounds: that Marxism, like Islam, is a Judeo-Christian heresy. We continue today to live, as we have lived for about 1,700 years, very largely in a context of Christian axioms.

What did Christianity tell people about their relations with the environment?

While many of the world's mythologies provide stories of creation, Greco-Roman mythology was singularly incoherent in this respect. Like Aristotle, the intellectuals of the ancient West denied that the visible world had had a beginning. Indeed, the idea of a beginning was impossible in the framework of their cyclical notion of time. In sharp contrast, Christianity inherited from Judaism not only a concept of time as non-repetitive and linear but also a striking story of creation. By gradual stages a loving and all-powerful God had created light and darkness, the heavenly bodies, the earth and all its plants, animals, birds, and fishes. Finally, God had created Adam and, as an afterthought, Eve to keep man from being lonely. Man named all the animals, thus establishing his dominance over them. God planned all of this explicitly for man's benefit and rule: no item in the physical creation had any purpose save to serve man's purposes. And, although man's body is made of clay, he is not simply part of nature: he is made in God's image.

Especially in its Western form, Christianity is the most anthropocentric religion the world has seen. As early as the second century both Tertullian and Saint Irenaeus of Lyons were insisting that when God shaped Adam he was foreshadowing the image of the incarnate Christ, the Second Adam. Man shares, in great measure, God's transcendence of nature. Christianity, in absolute contrast to ancient paganism and Asia's religions (except, perhaps, Zoroastrianism), not only established a dualism of man and nature, but also insisted that it is God's will that man exploit nature for his proper ends.

At the level of the common people this worked out in an interesting way. In Antiquity every tree, every spring, every stream, every hill had its own *genius loci*, its guardian spirit. These spirits were accessible to men, but were very unlike men; centaurs, fauns, and mermaids show their ambivalence. Before one cut a tree, mined a mountain, or dammed a brook, it was important to placate the spirit in charge of that particular situation, and to keep it placated. By destroying pagan animism, Christianity made it possible to exploit nature in a mood of indifference to the feelings of natural objects.

It is often said that for animism the Church substituted the cult of saints. True; but the cult of saints is functionally quite different from animism. The saint is not *in* natural objects; he may have special shrines, but his citizenship is in heaven. Moreover, a saint is entirely a man; he can be approached in human terms. In addition to saints, Christianity of course also had angels and demons inherited from Judaism and perhaps, at one remove, from Zoroastrianism. But these were all as mobile as the saints themselves. The spirits *in* natural objects, which formerly had protected nature from man, evaporated. Man's effective monopoly on spirit in this world was confirmed, and the old inhibitions to the exploitation of nature crumbled.

When one speaks in such sweeping terms, a note of caution is in order. Christianity is a complex faith, and its consequences differ in differing contexts. What I have said may well apply to the medieval West, where in fact technology made spectacular advances. But the Greek East, a highly civilized realm of equal Christian devotion, seems to have produced no marked technological innovation after the late seventh century, when Greek fire was invented. The key to the contrast may perhaps be found in a difference in the tonality of piety and thought which students of comparative theology find between the Greek and the Latin Churches. The

Greeks believed that sin was intellectual blindness, and that salvation was found in illumination, orthodoxy – that is, clear thinking. The Latins, on the other hand, felt that sin was moral evil, and that salvation was to be found in right conduct. Eastern theology has been intellectualist. Western theology has been voluntarist. The Greek saint contemplates; the Western saint acts. The implications of Christianity for the conquest of nature would emerge more easily in the Western atmosphere.

The Christian dogma of creation, which is found in the first clause of all the Creeds, has another meaning for our comprehension of today's ecologic crisis. By revelation, God had given man the Bible, the Book of Scripture. But since God had made nature, nature also must reveal the divine mentality. The religious study of nature for the better understanding of God was known as natural theology. In the early Church, and always in the Greek East, nature was conceived primarily as a symbolic system through which God speaks to men: the ant is a sermon to sluggards; rising flames are the symbol of the soul's aspiration. This view of nature was essentially artistic rather than scientific. While Byzantium preserved and copied great numbers of ancient Greek scientific texts, science as we conceive it could scarcely flourish in such an ambience.

However, in the Latin West by the early thirteenth century natural theology was following a very different bent. It was ceasing to be the decoding of the physical symbols of God's communication with man and was becoming the effort to understand God's mind by discovering how His creation operates. The rainbow was no longer simply a symbol of hope first sent to Noah after the Deluge: Robert Grosseteste, Friar Roger Bacon, and Theodoric of Freiberg produced startlingly sophisticated works on the optics of the rainbow, but they did it as a venture in religious understanding. From the thirteenth century onward, up to and including Leibnitz and Newton, every major scientist, in effect, explained his motivations in religious terms. Indeed, if Galileo had not been so expert an amateur theologian he would have got into far less trouble: the professionals resented his intrusion. And Newton seems to have regarded himself more as a theologian than as a scientist. It was not until the late eighteenth century that the hypothesis of God became unnecessary to many scientists.

It is often hard for the historian to judge, when men explain why they are doing what they want to do, whether they are offering real reasons or merely culturally acceptable reasons. The consistency with which scientists during the long formative centuries of Western science said that the task and the reward of the scientist was 'to think God's thoughts after him' leads one to believe that this was their real motivation. If so, then modern Western science was cast in a matrix of Christian theology. The dynamism of religious devotion, shaped by the Judeo-Christian dogma of creation, gave it impetus.

An alternative Christian view

We would seem to be headed toward conclusions unpalatable to many Christians. Since both *science* and *technology* are blessed words in our contemporary vocabulary, some may be happy at the notions, first, that, viewed historically, modern science is an extrapolation of natural theology and, second, that modern technology is at least partly to be explained as an Occidental, voluntarist realization of the Christian dogma of man's transcendence of, and rightful mastery over, nature. But, as we now recognize, somewhat over a century ago science and technology – hitherto quite separate activities – joined to give mankind powers which, to judge by many of the ecologic effects, are out of control. If so, Christianity bears a huge burden of guilt.

I personally doubt that disastrous ecologic backlash can be avoided simply by applying to our problems more science and more technology. Our science and technology have grown out of Christian attitudes toward man's relation to nature which are almost universally held not only by Christians and neo-Christians but also by those who fondly regard themselves as post-Christians. Despite Copernicus, all the cosmos rotates around our little globe. Despite Darwin, we are *not*, in our hearts, part of the natural process. We are superior to nature, contemptuous of it, willing to use it for our slightest whim. The newly elected Governor of California, like myself a churchman but less troubled than I, spoke for the Christian tradition when he said (as is alleged), 'when you've seen one redwood tree, you've seen them all'. To a Christian a tree can be no more than a physical fact. The whole concept of the sacred grove is alien to Christianity and to the ethos of the West. For nearly two millennia Christian missionaries have been chopping down sacred groves, which are idolatrous because they assume spirit in nature.

What we do about ecology depends on our ideas of the man–nature relationship. More science and more technology are not going to get us out of the present ecologic crisis until we find a new religion, or rethink our old one. The beatniks, who are the basic revolutionaries of our time, show a sound instinct in their affinity for Zen Buddhism, which conceives of the man–nature relationship as very nearly the mirror image of the Christian view. Zen, however, is as deeply conditioned by Asian history as Christianity is by the experience of the West, and I am dubious of its viability among us.

Possibly we should ponder the greatest radical in Christian history since Christ: Saint Francis of Assisi. The prime miracle of Saint Francis is the fact that he did not end at the stake, as many of his left-wing followers did. He was so clearly heretical that a General of the Franciscan Order, Saint Bonaventura, a great and perceptive Christian, tried to suppress the early accounts of Franciscanism. The key to an understanding of Francis is his belief in the virtue of humility – not merely for the individual but for man as a species. Francis tried to depose man from his monarchy over creation and set up a democracy of all God's creatures. With him the ant is no longer simply a homily for the lazy, flames a sign of the thrust of the soul toward union with God; now they are Brother Ant and Sister Fire, praising the Creator in their own ways as Brother Man does in his.

Later commentators have said that Francis preached to the birds as a rebuke to men who would not listen. The records do not read so: he urged the little birds to praise God, and in spiritual ecstasy they flapped their wings and chirped rejoicing. Legends of saints, especially the Irish saints, had long told of their dealings with animals but always, I believe, to show their human dominance over creatures. With Francis it is different. The land around Gubbio in the Apennines was being ravaged by a fierce wolf. Saint Francis, says the legend, talked to the wolf and persuaded him of the error of his ways. The wolf repented, died in the odour of sanctity, and was buried in consecrated ground.

What Sir Steven Runciman calls 'the Franciscan doctrine of the animal soul' was quickly stamped out. Quite possibly it was in part inspired, consciously or unconsciously, by the belief in reincarnation held by the Cathar heretics who at that time teemed in Italy and southern France, and who presumably had got it originally from India. It is significant that at just the same moment, about 1200, traces of metempsychosis are found also in western Judaism, in the Provençal *Cabbala*. But Francis held neither to transmigration of souls nor to pantheism. His view of nature and of man rested on a unique sort of pan-psychism of all things animate and inanimate, designed for the glorification of their transcendent Creator, who, in the ultimate gesture of cosmic humility, assumed flesh, lay helpless in a manger, and hung dying on a scaffold.

I am not suggesting that many contemporary Americans who are concerned about our ecologic crisis will be either able or willing to counsel with wolves or exhort birds. However, the present increasing disruption of the global environment is the product of a dynamic technology and science which were originating in the Western medieval world against which Saint Francis was rebelling in so original a way. Their growth cannot be understood historically apart from distinctive attitudes toward nature which are deeply grounded in Christian dogma. The fact that most people do not think of these attitudes as Christian is irrelevant. No new set of basic values has been accepted in our society to displace those of Christianity. Hence we shall continue to have a worsening ecologic crisis until we reject the Christian axiom that nature has no reason for existence save to serve man.

The greatest spiritual revolutionary in Western history, Saint Francis, proposed what he thought was an alternative Christian view of nature and man's relation to it: he tried to substitute the idea of the equality of all creatures, including man, for the idea of man's limitless rule of creation. He failed. Both our present science and our present technology are so tinctured with orthodox Christian arrogance toward nature that no solution for our ecologic crisis can be expected from them alone. Since the roots of our trouble are so largely religious, the remedy must also be essentially religious, whether we call it that or not. We must rethink and refeel our nature and destiny. The profoundly religious, but heretical, sense of the primitive Franciscans for the spiritual autonomy of all parts of nature may point a direction. I propose Francis as a patron saint for ecologists.

2

Biblical foundations for creation care[1]

Ronald J. Sider

Ronald J. Sider is President of Evangelicals for Social Action, and Professor of Theology and Culture at the Eastern Baptist Theological Seminary in Pennsylvania. He was one of the founders of the Evangelical Environmental Network, the publisher of Creation Care *magazine. His book* Rich Christians in an Age of Hunger *(1978) has been extremely influential in many countries.*

In March 1990, in Seoul, South Korea, I attended an international conference on Justice, Peace and the Integrity of Creation sponsored by the World Council of Churches. I heard many persuasive claims about the way Christians had distorted humanity's mandate to have dominion over the Earth – the consequence of these distortions being a ravaged creation. I became concerned, however, when I noticed that no-one had mentioned the fact that human beings have an exalted status within creation, in that they alone are created in the image of God.

So I proposed a one-sentence addition to the document we were debating. From the floor, I asked that we add a sentence affirming that, as we confess these misunderstandings, we nonetheless 'accept the biblical teaching that people alone have been created in the image of God'.

The drafting committee promptly accepted the addition but dropped the word 'alone'. I pointed out that this undercut the basic point. Are trees and toads also created in God's image? When the drafting committee remained adamant, I called for a vote. And the motion lost! At that moment, a majority of attendees at this important convocation were unwilling to say what historical, biblical theology has always affirmed: that human beings alone are created in the image of God.

As my experience illustrates, in today's environmental movement there is a lot of theological confusion. Actress Shirley MacLaine says we must declare that we are all gods. Disciplined but unchastened Catholic theologian Matthew Fox says we should turn from a theology centred on sin and redemption and develop a creation spirituality, with nature as our primary revelation and sin a distant memory. Australian philosopher Peter Singer says any claim that persons have a status different from monkeys and moles is 'speciesism'. Several decades ago historian Lynn White argued that it is precisely the Christian view of persons and nature that created the whole ecological mess (see pp. 31–42). Meanwhile, many evangelicals come close to celebrating the demise of the Earth, enthusiastically citing the decay as proof that the return of Christ is very near.

These and other factors will tempt evangelicals to ignore or denounce environmental concerns. But that would be a tragic mistake – for at least three reasons. First, because the danger is massive and urgent. Second, because there are evangelistic opportunities that arise out of environmental concern. And third, because if we do not offer biblical foundations for environmental action, we will have only ourselves to blame if environmental activists turn to other, finally inadequate, worldviews and religions. With wisdom and a renewed appreciation of the wholeness of God's plan for redemption, we can lead the way forward in the healing of our Earth.

Increasingly, people who care deeply about the environment are searching for deeper spiritual foundations to ground their crusade to save the planet.

The pilgrimage proceeds in many directions. Some environmentalists are exploring the spirituality of nature people and ancient Druidism; others are trying New Age religion or ancient Eastern monism. There is a growing consensus, expressed by Maurice Strong, Secretary General of the International Earth Summit in 1992, that some spiritual foundation is essential. Strong said the Rio decisions require 'deep moral, spiritual, and ethical roots if they are to be successfully implemented'.

In 1990, a group of renowned scientists signed an 'Open Letter to the Religious Community', urging religious people to join the movement to save the environment (p. 187). In their statement, the scientists acknowledged that the ecological threat is so great that we cannot avoid disaster unless the religious community joins the struggle.

That is beginning to happen in important ways. On Earth Day 1994, Christians and Jews in the United States mailed out environmental kits to 53,800 congregations all across the country. A wide range of activities followed in the next five years. This effort, and a wide range of related activities, are the work of the National Religious Partnership for the Environment. The Partnership is a coalition of four groups: the US Catholic Conference, the National Council of Churches, the Evangelical Environment Network, and the Coalition on Jewish Life and the Environment.

The major religious communities in this country have joined the battle. As a leader in the Evangelical Environmental Network (which publishes the quarterly *Creation Care* magazine) and chairperson of a two-day event that finalized the *Evangelical Declaration on the Care of Creation,* I can say that American Christians are committed to environmental concerns for the long haul.

But that does not mean that all Christians are environmentalists. Nor does it mean that the environmental movement has found the spiritual foundations it seeks. One central task for environmentalists in the next decade will be to listen carefully to each other in order to search further for ethical and spiritual foundations solid enough to sustain an enduring movement to save the planet. In that dialogue, we must respectfully share our deepest convictions, even when our viewpoints differ. An open, tolerant discussion of the major alternatives will help us more than will silent avoidance of religious differences or vacuous generalities. In that spirit, I share my own perspective as a contribution to the developing dialogue.

I want to put forward two theses. First, people who ground their faith in the Bible will, if they are consistent, be passionate environmentalists. Second, environmentalists searching eagerly for religious foundations might discover unexpected help in biblical faith.

Both claims may sound strange. Is not Christianity, as Lynn White suggested decades ago, the problem rather than the solution? Are not Christians who claim to be biblical the worst offenders? Is it not evangelical Christians who tell us that the world will end soon, and therefore we might as well use up our resources before God blows them to bits?

How then can today's Christians offer any hope? Many, I confess, including some of the most visible and vocal, do not. But the reason is not that a biblical framework is destructive to the environment. Rather, it is that many Christians who are not environmentalists, and many environmentalists who are not Christians, have not carefully attended to what the Bible says about the creation and the Creator.

Probably nothing is more important for the future of the environmental movement than a proper understanding of the material world and the relationship of people to the non-human creation.

Christians have sometimes ignored the significance of the body and the material world, focusing all their energy on preparing the soul for some future, immaterial, invisible existence in a spiritual heaven. Interestingly, there are striking parallels between such Christians and Eastern monists who tell us that the material world is an illusion to be escaped, so that we can discover the divine spark within and eventually merge with the All and lose all individual identity. It is hard to see how either view would be of much help to environmentalists. If the material world is evil or an illusion, why worry about it?

Biblical faith, however, is radically different. Every part of the material world comes from the loving hand of the Creator who calls it into being out of nothing and declares it very good. Unlike the Creator, the creation is finite and limited, but it is not an illusion. Nor is it the result of blind, materialistic chance, although the Creator lovingly nurtured it into existence over the course of a long evolutionary history.

In biblical faith, the material world is so good that the Creator of the galaxies actually became flesh once in the time of Caesar Augustus. Indeed, the material world is so good that not only did Jesus devote much time to restoring broken bodies, he also arose bodily from death and promised to return to complete his victory over every form of brokenness in persons, nature and civilization.

According to biblical faith, God's cosmic plan of restoration includes the whole creation, not just individual 'souls'. The apostle Paul says that at the end of history as we now experience it, Christ will return, not only to usher believers into a life of restored bodily existence in the presence of God, but also to restore the whole non-human creation. 'The creation itself will be set free from its bondage to decay and will obtain the freedom of the glory of the children of God' (Rom. 8:21, NRSV). In that restored earth, I expect to go sailing with my great-grandchildren on a replenished Aral Sea.

The last book of the Bible uses a beautiful metaphor about the tree of life growing beside an unpolluted river, pure as crystal, that purges human civilization of its brokenness and evil so that the glory and honour of the nations may enter into the holy city of the future (Rev. 21:22 – 22:2). Unlike

Christian Platonists and Hindu Monists who see the material world as an evil or as an illusion to escape, biblical people believe that it matters so much that the Creator will eventually restore its broken beauty. Knowing God's grand design, Christians can work to initiate now what God will later complete.

Few things are more controversial today than the status of persons in relationship to the non-human world. Some, including some Christians, suppose that the only purpose of the non-human world is to serve humanity. Therefore, they conclude, we can ravage and destroy species and ecological systems at will. A liveable-in environment cannot survive another century of such thinking. At the other extreme are those who reject any distinction between monkeys, moles and people, denouncing any claim to superior status for people as speciesism. If that is correct, then human civilization itself becomes impossible. What right have we to use plants and animals for our food and shelter if we are of no more importance than they?

Biblical faith offers another perspective. The Bible teaches both that the non-human creation has worth and significance, quite apart from its usefulness to humanity, and also that persons alone are created in God's image and called to be stewards of God's good garden.

Anyone who thinks God created the non-human world merely for the benefit of persons has not read the Bible carefully. God feeds the birds and clothes the lilies (Matt. 6:26–30). God watches over the deer hind in the mountains, counting the months of her pregnancy and watching over her when she gives birth, though she never encounters a human being (Job 39:1–2). In the story of the flood, God makes a covenant, not just with Noah and his family, but also with the non-human creation: 'I am establishing my covenant with you and your descendants after you, and with every living creature that is with you, the birds, the domestic animals and every animal of the earth' (Gen. 9:9–10, NRSV). Knowing that they all give joy to their Creator, Christians will treasure every species.

The independent worth of the non-human creation and humanity's interdependence with it do not, however, mean that we should forget another central biblical claim: human beings alone are created in the image of God, and we alone have been given a special dominion or stewardship of the Earth (Gen. 1:27–28). If one abandons that truth, the whole project of civilization crumbles.

Genesis 2:15 says God put people in the garden 'to work it and take care of it'. The word '*ābad*, translated as 'work', means 'to serve'. The related noun actually means 'slave' or 'servant'. The word *šāmar*, translated as 'take care of', suggests watchful care and preservation of the earth. (Psalm 121 repeatedly uses this same verb to describe the way the Lord unceasingly watches over his people.) We are to serve and watch lovingly over God's good garden, not rape it.

The Mosaic law offers explicit commands designed to prevent exploitation of the Earth. Every seventh year, for instance, the Israelites' land was to lie fallow because 'the land is to have a sabbath of rest' (Lev. 25:4).

Created in the divine image, we alone have been placed in charge of the Earth. At the same time, our dominion must be the gentle care of a loving gardener, not the callous exploitation of a self-centred lordling. So we should not wipe out species or waste the non-human creation. Only a careful, stewardly use of plants and animals by human beings is legitimate.

Biblical faith also provides a framework for dealing with the destructive rat race of unbridled consumption. The planet cannot sustain ten billion people living the kind of ever-expanding lifestyle that North Americans now demand. The Creator who made us, both body and soul, wants us to enjoy the gorgeous bounty of the material world. At the same time, we are created in such a way that human wholeness and fulfilment come not only from material things, but also from right relationships with neighbour and God. Both the call to care for our neighbour and the summons to sabbatical worship of God place limits on human acquisition and consumption. Material things are very good, but less important than spending time and enjoying right relationships with neighbour and God.

The eighteenth century abandoned the biblical worldview. The isolated, autonomous individual replaced God at the centre of reality. The scientific method became the only avenue to truth and reality.

We can measure an ever-increasing GNP and an expanding stock portfolio. We cannot easily measure the goodness of community in the extended family, or the value of caring for the neighbour, not to mention the value of a personal relationship with God. Frantically, each individual seeks fulfilment in more and more material things, even though our very nature makes it impossible for such things to satisfy our deepest needs. The destructive, unbridled consumerism of modern society is rooted in this narcissistic individualism and materialistic naturalism that flow from the Enlightenment. Biblical faith, on the other hand, provides a framework within which we can both enjoy material abundance and understand its limits.

I believe biblical faith provides a solid foundation for caring for the creation entrusted to us by the Creator. Perhaps if more Christians engaged in environmental practices that were consistent with biblical teaching, more environmentalists would be ready to explore again the claim that a biblical framework would offer our best hope for a comprehensive Earth-healing.

3

The making of the *Declaration*

Loren Wilkinson

Loren Wilkinson is Professor of Interdisciplinary Studies at Regent College, Vancouver, British Columbia. He prepared the initial draft of An Evangelical Declaration on the Care of Creation.

Like it or not, I have a unique relationship to *An Evangelical Declaration on the Care of Creation,* for I wrote the initial draft of the document, and worked closely with the people who are responsible for its final form. So I will try to say a bit about the personal, historical and theological milieu in which it was written.

I was invited to prepare an initial draft by the Evangelical Environmental Network after its first meeting at the Au Sable Environmental Studies Centre in the summer of 1993, following the Rio Earth Summit. Perhaps I was invited to do so because I had been the editor of both the original (1980) and the revised (1990) edition of *Earth-keeping,* a book which came out of a year-long interdisciplinary study of Christian environmental stewardship sponsored by Calvin College in 1977–78 (Wilkinson 1990). In any case, I drafted the first version of the *Declaration,* and circulated it (as was suggested) to Calvin DeWitt (see pp. 60–73) and Susan Drake Emmerich (see pp. 147–154). Cal is a biologist at the University of Wisconsin and director of the Au Sable Institute for Environmental Studies (and was also one of the original members of the Calvin College 'Earth-keeping' study); Susan, while working at the US State Department, had done crucial behind-the-scenes work with the UN in bringing about the 1993 Earth Summit.

Cal's suggestions fleshed out the document on the scientific side, and Susan's on the political and applied side. This augmented draft was then brought to a committee of several American evangelical leaders who met in an anonymous, windowless conference room in a hotel near Chicago's O'Hare Airport. A dozen or so people were present for this session: in addition to Cal and Susan, there were Kenneth Kantzer, a theologian (of Trinity Evangelical Divinity School, and a former editor of *Christianity Today*); Tom Oden (from Drew University); Ronald Sider, a theologian and ethicist (from Eastern Baptist Seminary) and author of *Rich Christians in an Age of Hunger* (and of the article on pp. 43–49), Steve Hayner, US director of Intervarsity; and one or two people from the editorial staff of *Christianity Today*.

We worked for a day on the document, engaging a little in the frustrating activity of group wordsmithing, but also (and more profitably) considerably refining and expanding the preamble (the nine opening paragraphs, down to 'Many concerned people') and the eleven concluding paragraphs, beginning 'Therefore we call upon Christians ...' The central sixteen paragraphs of theological foundation were polished and somewhat shortened but (unlike the opening and closing sections) were not changed substantially from the initial draft.

The *Declaration* in its present form was published in *Christianity Today* in 1994, and has since been fairly widely circulated, and affirmed by many evangelical Christian leaders. I am glad to have had a role in its drafting, and hope it continues to be of use. However, because I was so closely involved in its origin, it is a little hard for me to write critically of the document either positively or negatively; that work is done by others in this book. Let me make instead some observations, first on the *Declaration*'s cultural setting and, second, on its theological base, from the perspective of a North American Christian who has been involved in the 'environmental' discussion for the past thirty years.

To begin with, the timing of the *Declaration* indirectly reflects some crucial aspects of the environmental problem itself, and of the response to it in both the emerging global culture and the smaller evangelical subculture. The nature of the environmental problem is outlined briefly in early paragraphs, drawing on a popular, widely delivered talk by Cal DeWitt in which the creational resonance of the number seven was used to highlight the 'seven degradations of creation' (a version of this is included in this book on pp. 61–62).

A key phrase is 'that we are pressing against the finite limits God has set for creation'. One might well ask, '*When* did we begin pressing against those limits?' Or, to put it more precisely, 'Are the limits new?' The obvious answer seems to be 'no'. But if the created 'limits' remain the same, has the fundamental behaviour of the human race changed to bring us, in a new way, up against those limits?

Here the problem cannot be answered so neatly. In the list of 'seven degradations' only one, 'global toxification', could in any clear way be seen as 'new' in human history: the result of our ability to produce substances (many pesticides, chlorofluorocarbons, radioactive waste) which the recycling systems of the planet are unable to deal with. Yet even this manifestation of human increase in technical ingenuity is simply one late development in a steadily growing human repertoire of tools for using and modifying creation; it does not signal a fundamentally new human behaviour. Reflecting on the other 'degradations' – land and water degradation, deforestation, species extinction, etc. – makes clear that human beings have not fundamentally changed their relationship to creation to bring about this crisis.

There have been many technological changes which have accelerated (especially in the last hundred years) both the growth of the human population and the impact of ancient human behaviours. But the real source of the environmental movement is rather a change not in limits, nor in the behaviour of fallen humanity, but in our *perception*. To begin with, in the twentieth century we saw the disappearance of 'frontiers', the closing of the possibility of new empire, and a growing awareness of the limitation of the planet as 'resource'. A case could well be made that the two great wars – significantly, 'world' wars – in the first half of that century were the result of this growing frustration at the planet's limits.

But in the last half of the twentieth century, while our perception of limits continued to grow, it was matched by another kind of perception, one tinged more with awe than anxiety: that is, the awareness of the Earth as a kind of divine gift – a uniquely friendly place in a vast and inhospitable cosmos. This fundamentally *religious* perception of the Earth is symbolized powerfully by those photographs of the Earth from space: particularly, starting in the late 1960s, pictures of the misted green planet rising above the bone-white sterility of a lunar landscape. Those images of the Earth from space have become – as many have pointed out – almost a late-twentieth-century religious icon.

The change in perception symbolized by these pictures of the planet is probably irreversible in human experience. It has not, however, been matched by an irreversible change in human behaviour. The limits of the Earth have not changed; neither, in any fundamental way, has the human behaviour which challenges those limits. Which brings us to the immediate setting for this *Declaration*.

It grew, as already mentioned, out of a Christian response to the 1993 Earth Summit. As is clear in retrospect, that remarkable two-week meeting in Rio had much more to do with a global change in *perception* than with a global change in *behaviour*. The various political accords have been given lip-service, or simply ignored, and most of the trends which were noted with alarm at that meeting have only increased in the intervening years. What *has* changed is an awareness of a deep flaw in human nature, and a need for some sort of *religious* change to meet the problem. This awareness resulted, in the 1990s, in many movements which began to call for a new 'spirituality'. Many of those movements – including the Evangelical Environmental Network which sponsored the *Declaration* – are Christian.

It is easy to be cynical about these movements. Whether Christian or neo-pagan, they have had little impact on the growing engine of economic globalization, with its tendency to ignore the limits of creation in pursuit of the creation of wealth. In fact, a number of works by Christians have been written since the Earth Summit, defending such 'wealth creation' and decrying any attempt – like the one represented by this *Declaration* – to limit it in the name of Christianity. Widespread awareness of environmental problems seems to come and go depending mainly on the appearance in the media of environmentally related disasters. But (in T. S. Eliot's words) 'mankind cannot bear very much reality'. So despite the appearance of various 'Earth' or 'creation' spiritualities, human behaviour has not changed much. We continue to engage in the 'seven degradations' mentioned in the *Declaration*'s opening paragraphs.

Christians with interests in the health of creation need also to recognize that their concern may simply be part of a larger cultural movement to think religiously about the Earth; in this they need to beware the tendency simply to tag along after cultural trends.

But there is another way to regard these 'creation spiritualities' – and this *Declaration*. Christians have always affirmed that there is a message-character to creation: word about the glory of the Creator has gone out 'into all the earth'. It is undeniable that the message has been garbled and confused by the ancient lure of worshipping the Creature rather than the Creator (Rom. 1:25); but it seems clear also that something of that message has got through the 'jamming' effect of living in an increasingly arrogant and triumphalist human world.

There is great promise and great danger – for Christians, for 'the environmental movement' and for the Earth – in this religious response. The promise is obvious: the growing human sense of the Earth as a divine gift can only lead to greater care of the Earth. And it *should* lead to a greater worship of the Creator. In the fact that it does not always – or often – lead to such worship lies the danger. For Christians, the danger is the tendency to see all environmental concerns as a thin veil for various forms of neo-paganism: worship of nature, or 'the great Goddess'. The tragedy is that this reaction against false religions leads them to understand the salvation proclaimed in the Christian gospel in a dangerously, and unbiblically, narrow way.

Typical of this reactionary narrowing of the gospel is the letter I received from a Christian minister in response to his hearing a talk in which I had suggested that creation was included in God's plan of salvation. He wrote: 'Christ's redemption is always in purchasing the chosen or elect from their trespasses ... the redemption of the earth from its groaning will be its vaporization and replacement. Its value is in providing our habitation; it is a variable, we are the constant with God. Praise the Lord that his promise is made so clear to those that want to hear.'

Often accompanying this kind of attitude is the conviction that since neo-pagan environmentalists seek to care for the Earth by limiting the unimpeded operation of the global economic system, the only Christian response is to support the purest form of *laissez-faire* capitalism. Several books taking this approach have been published, and widely read, by Christians in recent years.

For the non-Christian community of environmentally concerned people, this visible opposition by many Christians to any initiative towards caring for the Earth has the tragic result of causing them, in their increasingly religious quest for a spiritual foundation, to turn anywhere *except* to the God revealed in Jesus.

But of course this is not the whole story of the Christian response. On the opposite side is the growing movement among many Christians which lies behind this *Declaration* – the Evangelical Environmental Network –

and those many other movements within Christian orthodoxy towards an ethic of creation care. The most encouraging thing about this movement is that it is not a sort of faddish addition, but that it proceeds from a recovery of the very heart of the Christian gospel. The theological centre of the *Declaration* reflects some of this new discovery of the ancient, biblical understanding of God's radical, self-giving love for the whole creation. Perhaps the theological centrality of those ideas could have been even clearer in the *Declaration*.

The quickest way to sum up the theological recovery which lies at the heart of the *Declaration* is to say that it reflects a renewed understanding of the importance, in Christian faith and practice, of the doctrine of the Trinity. In the immediate sense, the renewed importance of this doctrine is due to work by contemporary theologians, many of them British: the Torrances – Thomas, James and Alan – Colin Gunton and Jeremy Begbie; but also continental thinkers, such as Jürgen Moltmann (as in the 1984–85 Gifford Lectures, *God in Creation*; see also pp. 107–113), and the wonderfully titled work by John Zizioulas, *Being as Communion*.

The theological work of many people (including myself) in attempting to articulate a Christian framework for the care of creation has often been impeded by the difficulty of maintaining a biblical balance between God's transcendence and God's immanence. If there has indeed been (as so many have argued) a negative influence of Christians on the health of the planet, it has undoubtedly resulted from an exaggeration – or rather, a misunderstanding – of God's transcendence. Such a misunderstanding has sometimes resulted in a kind of deism, leading us to regard the cosmos, and life itself, as nothing more than a kind of well-constructed machine with which God has little or no ongoing relationship. It has also contributed to a misunderstanding of what it means to be made in God's image – a misunderstanding which has exaggerated both our own sense of detachment from the rest of creation, and our sense of power over it.

Many religious (including some nominally Christian) attempts to correct this overemphasis on God's transcendence have resulted in an overemphasis on God's immanence. Much 'ecofeminist' theology, along with the 'creation spirituality' movement associated with people such as Matthew Fox and Thomas Berry, has, it seems to me, erred in this direction.

A proper understanding of God as Trinity protects us from both these errors. Jürgen Moltmann makes this particularly clear:

The Trinitarian concept of creation binds together God's transcendence and his immanence. The one-sided stress on God's transcendence in relation to the world led to deism, as with Newton. The one-sided stress on God's immanence in the world led to pantheism, as with Spinoza. The Trinitarian concept of creation integrates the elements of truth in monotheism and pantheism. God, having created the world, also dwells in it, and conversely the world which he has created exists in him. This is a concept which can really only be thought and described in Trinitarian terms (Moltmann 1985: 98).

This closeness of God to creation is abundantly clear in Scripture, and it was recognized clearly by early Christian thinkers. Irenaeus, for example, writes in the second century:

For the Creator of the world is truly the Word of God: and this is our Lord, who in the last times was made man, existing in this world, and who, in an invisible manner contains all things created, and is inherent in the entire creation, since the Word of God governs and arranges all things; and therefore He came to His own in a visible manner, and was made flesh, and hung upon the tree, that He might sum up all things in Himself.

Two centuries later Athanasius writes, in *On the Incarnation*:

We will begin, then, with the creation of the world and with God its Maker, for the first fact that you must grasp is this: *the renewal of creation has been wrought by the Self-same Word Who made it in the beginning.* There is thus no inconsistency between creation and salvation; for the One Father has employed the same Agent for both works, effecting the salvation of the world through the same Word Who made it at the first.

Both of these ancient Christian thinkers take seriously the basic Christian claim that Jesus was God. Thus they do not ignore the many New Testament passages (as in John 1:1ff., Col. 1:7ff., Heb. 1:1–2; Eph. 1:10; etc.) which stress the fundamental relationship of Christ and creation. That understanding of the relationship of Christ to creation complements and reinforces the Old Testament understanding of the Spirit of God in creation (as in, for example, Ps. 104:30), and does so in the light of the clear New Testament teaching of the *communion* of Father, Son and Spirit into which we are graciously invited.

The result of this recovered understanding of the Trinity is not only a clearer picture of the triune God's closeness to creation, but a deeper sense of the centrality of *communion* to creation itself. Catherine La Cugna, in her study of the Trinity called *God For Us*, puts it this way:

> Indeed, Trinitarian theology is *par excellence* a theology of relationship: God to us, we to God, we to each other. The doctrine of the Trinity affirms that the 'essence' of God is relational, other-ward, that God exists as diverse persons united in a communion of freedom, love and knowledge ... the focus of the doctrine of the Trinity is the communion between God and ourselves (La Cugna 1993: 243).

Colin Gunton, in his important work, *The One, The Three, and the Many* makes the same point, but broadens the scope of relationality to the whole universe:

> Of the universe as a whole we should conclude that it is marked by relationality ... All things are what they are by being particulars constituted by many and various forms of relation ... all created people and things are marked by their coming from and returning to the God who is himself, in his essential and inmost being, a being in relation (Gunton 1991).

This understanding of the centrality of *communion* to the nature of both Creator and creation has a profound implication for our understanding both of our relationship to God, and of our task in creation. The Cambridge theologian Jeremy Begbie, writing specifically about the arts, expresses eloquently this truth that creation is not left out of our restored relationship to the triune God, but that God's very relational nature ought to shape what we do:

> The God who calls us to cultivate the earth is not an impersonal Monad of absolute singularity, but the triune God who *is* love in his

very heart. His very being is relational; he is ecstatic love, love that always goes out to the other. His relation to the creation is thus not to be described in terms of logical necessity (as in pantheism or monism) or naked omnipotence (the tendency of the Calvinist tradition) but in terms of personal commitment and faithfulness. This in turn will affect the way in which we perceive human culture. A responsible developing of the earth depends on refusing to see creation outside its relation to the divine love. Moreover, the Son has taken flesh and, as it were, offered creation back to the Father in his own humanity, and now through the Holy Spirit invites us to share in the task of bringing creation to praise and magnify the Father in and through him (Begbie 1991: 181).

A final insight which this renewed Trinitarian understanding opens up to us is a deep sense of the costly love of the Creator. To quote Moltmann again:

God 'withdraws himself from himself to himself' in order to make creation possible. His creative activity outwards is preceded by this humble divine self-restriction. In this sense God's self-humiliation does not begin merely with creation, inasmuch as God commits himself to this world; it begins beforehand, and is the presupposition that makes creation possible. God's creative love is grounded in his humble, self-humiliating, love. This self-restricting love is the beginning of that self-emptying of God which Philippians 2 sees as the divine mystery of the Messiah. Even in order to create heaven and earth, God emptied himself of his all-plenishing omnipotence, and as Creator took upon himself the form of a servant (Moltmann 1985: 88).

These biblical and theological insights lie behind such statements in the *Declaration* as:

Our creating God is prior to and other than creation, yet intimately involved with it, upholding each thing in its freedom and all things in relationships of intricate complexity.

God the Creator is relational in very nature ... Likewise, the creation which God intended is a symphony of individual creatures in harmonious relationship.

The presence of the kingdom of God is marked not only by renewed fellowship with God, but also by renewed harmony and justice between people, and by renewed harmony and justice between people and the rest of the created world.

There is much more *thinking* to do on the implications of Trinitarian theology for our relationship to both Creator and creation. More important, we need to demonstrate in our lives, individually and communally, the healing and reconciliation brought about by Christ. We have far to go; my hope is that this *Declaration* has been, and will continue to be, some small help on that way.

4

Creation's environmental challenge to evangelical Christianity[1]

Calvin B. DeWitt

Calvin B. DeWitt is Professor of Environmental Studies at the University of Wisconsin-Madison and Director of the Au Sable Institute of Environmental Studies. He has been a pioneer and inspiration of Christian environmentalism in North America, and has written and edited many key works, including The Environment and the Christian *(1991),* Missionary Earthkeeping *(1992, with Ghillean Prance),* Earthwise *(1994) and* Caring for Creation *(1998).*

> For God sent not his Son into the world to condemn the world, but that the world through him might be saved. He that believeth in him, shall not be condemned ... But he that doeth truth, cometh to the light, that his deeds may be made manifest, that they are wrought according to God (John 3:17, 18a, 21, Geneva Bible).[2]

Creation's integrity and violation

'The time has come ... for destroying those who destroy the earth.' This pronouncement of Revelation 11:18 is one that made little sense to anyone until recently. It has been largely neglected in pulpit and pew, and has had little to do with people's 'manifest deeds' – the way people conduct their lives. This ominous judgment – proclaimed at the sound of the last trumpet – has been unheeded for apparently good reason. For how could human beings possibly destroy the Earth? How could people abuse their stewardship responsibility on such a scale? And why would people ever use their authority over creation (Gen. 1:28) to destroy creation – thereby to negate their own dominion! And, even if they did abuse their God-given stewardship of creation, certainly people would never gain enough power to destroy the Earth!

Recently, however, we have been given reason to ponder the composite immensity of human power. Every day we learn about new destructions of land and creatures. And, while some reports are dramatized and overstated, professional scientific literature time and again describes new and increasing instances of environmental degradation. In calm and dispassionate scientific language, accounts in refereed technical literature are building a description of Earth's destruction. These accounts, taken together, announce what would have been unbelievable a century ago. Human beings have become the predominant destructive force on Earth. With power of hands and minds amplified by machines, our impact exceeds that of great floods, hurricanes and earthquakes. The time has come when we can envisage the end of nature; the time has come to realize that we are able to destroy the Earth.

Seven degradations of creation

An analysis of the scientific literature produces a picture of Earth's destruction describable as 'seven degradations of creation'.[3] These degradations, all of which interact, include:

1. *Alteration of Earth's energy exchange* with the sun, which results in accelerated global warming and destruction of the Earth's protective ozone shield.[4]

2. *Land degradation*, which destroys land by erosion, salinization and desertification, and reduces available land for creatures and crops.[5]

3. *Deforestation*, which annually removes some 100,000 square kilometres of primary forest – an area the size of Iceland – and degrades an equal amount by over-use.[6]

4. *Species extinction*, which finds more than three species of plants and animals eliminated from Earth each day.[7]

5. *Water-quality degradation*, which defiles groundwater, lakes, rivers and oceans.[8]

6. *Waste generation and global toxification*, which result from atmospheric and oceanic circulation of the materials that people inject into the air and water.[9]

7. *Human and cultural degradation*, which threatens and eliminates longstanding human communities that have lived sustainably and cooperatively with creation, and eliminates a multitude of longstanding varieties of food and garden plants.[10]

Seven provisions of creation

These degradations contrast with what can be called 'seven provisions of the Creator' upon which creation, all creatures and human life depend. These seven provisions – many of which are celebrated in Psalm 104 – are indicative of the remarkable integrity and beauty that have engendered awe, wonder and respect for the Creator and creation throughout the ages. These provisions – given here in parallel with the seven degradations – are:

1. *Regulation of Earth's energy exchange with the sun*, which keeps Earth's temperatures at a level supportive of life through the longstanding greenhouse effect, and which protects life from the sun's lethal ultraviolet radiation by filtering sunlight through the stratospheric ozone layer.

2. *Biogeochemical cycles and soil-building processes*, which cycle oxygen, carbon, water and other vital materials through living things and their habitats and build life-supporting soils and soil structure.

3. *Ecosystem energy transfer and materials recycling*, which continually energizes life on Earth and incessantly allocates life-sustaining materials.

4. *Water purification systems of the biosphere*, which distil, filter and purify surface waters and ground water upon which all life depends.

5. *Biological and ecological fruitfulness*, which supports and maintains the rich biodiversity of life on Earth by means of responsive and adaptive physiologies and behaviours.

6. *Global circulations of water and air*, which distribute water, oxygen, carbon dioxide and other vital materials between living systems across the planet.

7. *Human ability to learn from creation and live in accord with its laws*, which makes it possible for people to live sustainably on Earth and safeguard the creation.[11]

Creation's testimony

These and God's many other provisions in creation convincingly proclaim God's love for the world. Creation's telling of God's glory and love is echoed by Scripture's testimony: God lovingly provides the rains and cyclings of water, provides food for the creatures, fills people's hearts with joy and satisfies the Earth (Ps. 104:10–18; Acts 14:17). It is through this manifest love and wisdom that creation declares God's glory and proclaims the work of the Creator's hands (Ps. 19:1). The evangelical words of creation permeate the universe (Ps. 19:1; Rom. 1:20), and from the very beginning creation's witness to God's integrity and love for the world has been pervasive; its voice has gone out clearly through all the Earth. Creation's evangelical declaration is so forceful that God's eternal power is clearly seen and God's divinity is manifest, leaving everyone without excuse (Rom. 1:20; Ps. 19:1). *Just as people turn a deaf ear to the gospel*

But this powerful statement by creation itself is threatened. First, people *a presents to the church* are increasingly alienated from creation and its testimony. This alienation comes in part from their increasing separation from the natural world; for example, fewer and fewer people are needed in agriculture, so they move to expanding cities whose growing inner cores often displace and destroy nature. It also comes from the disconnection of human causes from environmental effects, as happens when people come to believe that food comes from a shop and petrol from a pump. Increasingly, this alienation also comes from a diminishing of creation's testimony through environmental degradation, as when once-inspiring rivers supporting diverse life are transformed into sewers, or when formerly clear skies are obscured by air pollutants. With this increasing estrangement comes complicit involvement in creation's degradation and even energetic work and action that destroy creation. Thus, the longstanding evangelical witness of creation is abandoned, muted and silenced, accompanied by even greater environmental degradation, in a continuing downward spiral.

Distancing of Redeemer from Creator

Correspondingly, in many churches God as Creator has been distanced from Christ as Redeemer. In the view of some, God has become only the one who saves, not the one who created and sustains the world, not the one who expects us to be imaging God in our care of creation. For some –

under the continuing influence of the Gnosticism that infected the early church – God has become the one who saves us out of creation.[12] This distancing of Saviour from Creator has gone so far in some minds that belief in the Creator has been reduced to words without deeds. Mimicking the absurd prospect that Rembrandt-praising art critics might somehow find it acceptable to trample Rembrandt paintings while honouring Rembrandt's name, some Creator-praising people now trample creation while proclaiming Christ's name. Having become distant from the Creator and creation, some Christians comfortably have neglected creation's evangelical testimony, and even assist in bringing creation's degradation.

Such behaviour, while distressing, is not surprising, say the Scriptures. Early on, the Bible tells us, people chose to go their own way, alienating themselves from God and from the consequences of their sin (Gen. 1 – 11). Human beings are described as prone to do anything within their capacity, rather than seeking to do what is right. People are more likely to do what they imagine rather than to do the truth; rather than to make belief in God manifest in their deeds (cf. John 3:16–21). And so today, what directs human behaviour is not so much what *should* be done as what *can* be done, reflecting God's concern at Babel that 'nothing they plan to do will be impossible for them' (Gen. 11:6). Breaking down the constraints of stewardship – discarding of the biblical principle of caring for creation and keeping the Garden – some pursue the possible instead of the right, and relish darkness instead of the light (John 3:19), bringing about the destruction of the Earth. Forsaking godliness, people may seek to become gods. In contrast with the teachings of 1 Timothy 6:6–21 where we are admonished to seek godliness with contentment as our great gain, they regard profit in terms of how much they can extract and take from creation. The creation groans; they destroy the Earth.

Ignoring the message of Revelation 11:18 – neglecting to love, keep and care for the world – means forsaking everlasting life. Neglecting to love the world, people degrade and destroy the world. Failing to hear God's word and creation's testimony, they degrade creation. Violating the laws the rest of creation observes, and failing to hear modern prophets who merely describe the present, people plunge toward destruction of Earth and thus also themselves. Using godly, technical and political language, they fail to see and hear; they deny the reality of creation's present degradation. Many of their leaders read the polls, and then tell the people what they want to hear.

At another time of environmental degradation, six centuries before Christ, Jeremiah described a similar undoing of creation: 'I looked at the earth, and it was formless and empty; and at the heavens, and their light was gone. I looked at the mountains and they were quaking; all the hills were swaying. I looked, and there were no people; every bird in the sky had flown away. I looked, and the fruitful land was a desert; all its towns lay in ruins before the LORD, before his fierce anger' (Jer. 4:23–26). Neglecting to do God's will in the world is not new, and its environmental consequences have been known for over two thousand years (cf. Jer. 5:22–23, 31; 8:7).

God's love for the world

But the Scriptures assure us that God loves the world (John 3:16). Admonishing people to choose life (Deut. 30:19), God offers a luminous alternative to destruction: everlasting life (John 3:16). While those who destroy the Earth themselves will be destroyed, those who truly believe in the Creator, Sustainer and Reconciler of all things will not. Those who believe in the one through whom the world was made, the one who holds the world together, the one who reconciles the world and all things to himself, will receive the gift of everlasting life. To believe in this one is to honour and to follow Jesus Christ.

How does one follow the Creator of all things, the Author of creation that God repeatedly declares good in Genesis 1? How does one follow the Sustainer of all things, the Provider for creation, the Integrator of all things? How does one follow the Saviour who takes whatever is degraded in the world God loves and makes it right again?

Biblical principles for creation stewardship

How to follow Jesus – the Creator, Sustainer and Reconciler of all creation – is something we learn both from the Scriptures and from the working out of the love of God in creation. A number of biblical principles can be identified to help bring disciples of Jesus Christ into proper relationship to creation.[13] These principles are:

1. *We must keep the creation as God keeps us.* The Lord blesses us and keeps us (Num. 6:24–26); we in turn are expected to keep the Earth (Gen. 2:15). As God's keeping of us is a loving, caring, nurturing and sustaining keeping, so must be ours of creation. Imaging God – exercising dominion

in the manner of Christ (Phil. 2:5–8) – we join our Creator in keeping creation (cf. Gen. 1:28; Deut. 17:18–20), caring for the land as God does, keeping our eyes continually upon it (Deut. 11:11–12). 'He makes springs pour water into the ravines ... They give water to all the beasts of the field ... The birds of the air nest by the waters; they sing among the branches ... the earth is satisfied by the fruit of his work' (Ps. 104:10–13). And so too should it be satisfied by ours.

2. *We must be disciples of the Last Adam, not of the First Adam.* We are part of a lineage that has fallen short of the glory of God (Rom. 3:23). 'But', affirm the Scriptures, 'Christ has indeed been raised from the dead ... as in Adam all die, so in Christ all will be made alive' (1 Cor. 15:20–22). 'For God was pleased to have all his fulness dwell in him, and through him to reconcile to himself all things' (Col. 1:19–20). As disciples of the one by whom 'all things were made', and through whom 'all things hold together', we participate in undoing the work of the First Adam, bringing restoration and reconciliation to *all things* (John 1 and Col. 1; 1 Cor. 15 and Rom. 5; Is. 43:18–21, Isa. 65 and Col. 1:19–20) (Manahan 1991).

3. *We must not press creation relentlessly, but must provide for its Sabbath rests.* As human beings and animals are to be given their Sabbaths, so also must the land be given its Sabbath rests (Exod. 20:8–11; 23:10–12). People, land and creatures must not be relentlessly pressured. 'If you follow my decrees ... I will send you rain in its season, and the ground will yield its crops and the trees of the field their fruit' (Lev. 26:3). Otherwise, the land will be laid waste, only then to 'have the rest it did not have during the sabbaths you lived in it' (Lev. 26:34–35)!

4. *We may enjoy, but not destroy, the grace of God's good creation.* The abundant gifts and fruitfulness of God's creation were not enough for Adam or his seed: in pressing for more and yet more there is even a willingness to destroy creation's sustaining fruitfulness. Our Sovereign Lord says: 'Is it not enough for you to feed on the good pasture? Must you also trample the rest of your pasture with your feet? Is it not enough for you to drink clear water? Must you also muddy the rest with your feet?' (Ezek. 34:18; see also Deut. 20:19; 22:6).

5. *We must seek first the kingdom, not self-interest.* This, then is how you should pray, 'Our Father in heaven, hallowed be your name, your kingdom come, your will be done on earth ...' (Matt. 6:9–10). It is tempting to follow the example of those who accumulate great gain, to creation's detriment. But the Scriptures assure us: 'Trust in the LORD and do good; dwell in the

land and enjoy safe pasture ... those who hope in the LORD will inherit the land' (Ps. 37:3, 9; Matt. 5:5). Fulfilment is a *consequence* of seeking the kingdom (Matt. 6:33; Zerbe 1991).

6. *We must seek contentment as our great gain.* The fruitfulness and grace of the Garden – the gifts of creation – did not satisfy Adam and subsequent generations (Gen. 3 – 11). Even as God promised not to forsake them, they chose to go their own way – squeezing ever more from creation. Our Creator wants us to pray: 'Turn my heart towards your statutes and not towards selfish gain' (Ps. 119:36). Paul, who had learned the secret of being content (Phil. 4:12b), writes: 'godliness with contentment is great gain ...' (1 Tim. 6:6–21; also see Heb. 13:5).

7. *We must not fail to act on what we know is right.* Knowing God's requirements for stewardship is not enough; they must be practised, or they do absolutely no good. Hearing, discussing, singing and contemplating God's message is not enough. We hear from our neighbours, 'Come and hear the message that has come from the LORD.' And they come, 'but they do not put them into practice. With their mouths they express devotion, but their hearts are greedy for unjust gain. Indeed, to them you are nothing more than one who sings love songs with a beautiful voice and plays an instrument well, for they hear your words but do not put them into practice' (Ezek. 33:30–32; see also Luke 6:46–49). Believing on God's Son (John 3:16), we must *do* the truth, making God's love for the world evident in our own deeds, energetically engaging in work and action that are in accord, harmony and fellowship with God, and God's sacrificial love (John 3:21).

Following the Creator, Sustainer and Reconciler of all creation is much more than reading – or even acting upon – these seven biblical principles. But they can bring us more deeply into the Scriptures and into contact with God's wider creation. From this greater penetration and broader comprehension of God's word and world we can become better disciples of Jesus Christ. No doubt, we all are guilty – for 'all have sinned and come short of the glory of God' – but our work is done out of joy and gratitude to God. For we have God's forgiveness – not forgiveness that gives licence to continue in sin 'that grace may abound', but rather forgiveness that permits joyful service in doing God's work in the world God loves so much. Joyful and grateful for God's love for us and the world, we expectantly pray, 'Thy kingdom come, Thy will be done, On earth ...'

Stumbling-blocks to creation's care and keeping

There are troublesome stumbling-blocks in the way of creation-keeping discipleship. All of us know of these stumbling-blocks and most of us have stumbled over them, thereby denying ourselves the experience of full stewardship under God. Some of these we have invented ourselves and others have been devised by our friends. We must identify these to clear the way for doing the service to which we are called. What are these stumbling-blocks?

1. *This world is not my home. I'm just passing through.* (Since we are headed for heaven anyway, why take care of creation?) It is true that those who believe on Jesus Christ (as Creator, Sustainer, Reconciler and Redeemer), will receive the gift of everlasting life. This everlasting life began with our birth and includes the here-and-now. And we in the here-and-now take care of our bodies, our teeth and our hair, even though 'the length of our days is seventy years – or eighty ...' (Ps. 90:10). Similarly, we take care of our buildings, even though the largest of these – the skyscrapers – are constructed with a demolition plan on file (to allow their safe destruction a hundred years or more later). Perhaps our learning how to take care of things in this moment of eternity is important for the care of things with which we will be entrusted later? Revelation 11:18 and other biblical teachings on care and keeping of creation certainly move in this direction. I have heard this summed up: 'We should so behave on earth that heaven is not a shock to us!'

2. *Caring for creation gets us too close to the New Age movement.* (Isn't concern for the environment and working for a better world what the New Age movement is all about? I don't want people to think I am a New Ager.) The Bible, of course, is about the kingdom of God, not the New Age movement. For thousands of years now, believers have looked forward to the coming of the kingdom of God and it is for this they continue to look when they pray, 'Thy kingdom come ...' Many of those in the New Age movement have never been told of the kingdom of God and, not having received the gospel, are doing what they can to invent their own. As the apostle Paul did for the people on Mars Hill in Athens – connecting their altar to the unknown god to the living God – so also should we do for the people in the New Age movement. We need to tell them that the new age they seek is the kingdom of God, bringing them the Good News: '... how can they hear without someone preaching to them?' (Rom. 10:14b).

3. *Respecting creation gets us too close to pantheism.* (If you care for plants and animals, and especially if you value the keeping of endangered species, you are close to worshipping them as gods.) Pantheism and panentheism are growing problems and (surprisingly in this age of science) worship of creatures is increasingly practised. Thus, we must be careful to worship the Creator, and not the creatures; we must be clear in our conveying the good news that God is the Creator and that the awe and wonder we develop from the study of creation is to be directed not at creation but at its Creator. As Paul teaches in Romans 1:25 and Luke in Acts 14:14–18, it is necessary to make this distinction. But this problem does not mean that we may deny or avoid taking care of creation. The example of Noah is instructive to us here: Noah cares for the creatures, and preserves the species endangered by the flood not because they are gods, but because God required it of him to keep the various species and kinds alive on the Earth.

4. *We need to avoid anything that looks like political correctness.* (Being 'politically correct' these days tends to mean being pro-abortion and pro-environment.) The Ku Klux Klan – a racist organization in the United States – uses the symbol of the cross in its terrorizing activities. Does this mean that Christians should no longer use the symbol of the cross on their churches? Some New Age people use the symbol of the rainbow in their literature. Does this mean that Christians who know this to be the sign of God's covenant with 'every living creature on earth' (Gen. 9:1–17) should stop using this symbol in their educational materials? People who identify themselves as 'politically correct' may advocate saving uneconomic species from extinction. Does this mean that there can be no new Noahs who, in response to God's call to save species from extinction, will act to preserve God's living creatures? Not only must we, as the children's hymn says, 'Dare to be a Daniel, dare to stand alone', but we also must 'Dare to be a Noah', even when we find ourselves complementing the work of a thousand unbelieving Noahs.

5. *There are too many worldly people out there doing environmental things.* (If people who don't share my beliefs in God and Jesus Christ are working to save the Earth, I know it can't be right for me.) God called Cyrus into divine service. We read in Isaiah 45 that unbelieving Cyrus was anointed to do God's work. Often, if God's people are unwilling or unable to do God's work, God sees to it that the work gets done nonetheless. And so, if there are some worldly people out there clearly doing God's work, it must

not be used to excuse ourselves from our God-given task as stewards of God's creation.

6. *Caring for creation will lead to world government.* (If we tackle global environmental problems, won't we have to cooperate with other nations, which will help set the stage for world government?) There is no doubt that cooperation will be necessary in order to address many of our environmental problems. Migrating birds, for example, do not recognize international boundaries; therefore their care requires cooperation. That this does not have to lead to world government is illustrated by the work of the International Crane Foundation, through whose work cooperation has been achieved between Russia and China and between North Korea and South Korea, in the keeping of wetland habitats and birds.

7. *Before you know it we will have to support abortion.* (Because of the relationship between environmental degradation and growing human population, we will soon find ourselves having to accept abortion as a solution to environmental problems.) Our obligation and privilege to care for God's creation does not give us licence to use whatever means we have at our disposal to address environmental problems. The fact that many people use abortion and justify it in terms of the need to reduce population growth does not mean that people who are convicted of a God-given responsibility of stewardship cannot proceed to take care of the Earth, including population problems.

8. *I don't want to be an extremist or alarmist.* (I want to be considered normal and not some kind of prophet of gloom and doom.) Gloom and doom are not necessary components of the message that needs to be brought to people about caring for creation. Frightening ourselves into action is far less desirable than caring for creation out of a love for the Creator and in gratitude and joy in keeping the Earth. As for being called an alarmist, is it wrong to sound the fire alarm when a building is burning? In many cases today it may be necessary to sound the alarm, just as did the prophets in their day.

9. *Dominion means what it says – oppressive domination.* (I think the Bible says that we have the right to destroy things that get in our way; that's what dominion is all about.) Many, particularly critics of Christianity, have pointed to Genesis 1:28 to show that the Bible is the root cause of environmental problems (see Lynn White's article, pp. 31–42). That this verse has been used in isolation from the rest of the Scriptures cannot be denied. But dominion as outright oppression is not advocated or condoned

by the Scriptures. First, the Genesis 1:28 passage gives the blessing and mandate to people before the fall. Second, this passage must be understood in the context of the rest of the Bible. If this is done, one must come to the conclusion that dominion means responsible stewardship, to which the biblical principles presented in this chapter attest. The Christian model for dominion is the example of Jesus Christ, who, given all dominion, and 'Who, being in very nature God ... made himself nothing, taking the very nature of a servant ... [and] humbled himself and became obedient to death – even death on a cross' (Phil. 2:6–8).

10. *People are more important than the environment.* (I'm for people, and that means that people are more important than saving species of plants and animals – if anything is endangered it is people, not furbished louseworts or snail darters.) This is an often-heard rationalization for not saving living species threatened with extinction. Our question here should be, 'What does the Bible teach?' We have an actual instance in the account of the flood given in Genesis 6 – 9. We need to ask, 'Who perishes, and who is saved?' Are species less important than individual people? Is the environment of people less important than the people this environment supports? God respects the environment so much that God calls heaven and Earth as witnesses against people (Deut. 30:19), witnesses to the fact that God has set before them the choice and admonishes them to choose life.

Then what must we do?

A challenge confronts us from the ongoing and accelerating degradation of the Earth, from the Scriptures that require us to keep the Earth, and from stumbling-blocks that prevent many evangelical Christians from taking action. Having set forth the challenge that confronts us, we now are prepared to ask, 'Then what must we do?'

The simple (yet profound) response to this question appears to be this: love God as Redeemer and Creator; acknowledge God's love for the world, and act upon this by following Jesus who creates, upholds and reconciles all things.

But most people have been alienated from the Creator and God's creation, and thus it is difficult to love, uphold and make right a world that we really do not know. Thus many will first have to become aware of creation and its God-declared goodness. From this awareness, we can move to appreciation, and from appreciation we can move to stewardship. This can be described using the following framework:

1. awareness (seeing, identifying, naming, locating);
2. appreciation (tolerating, respecting, valuing, esteeming, cherishing); and
3. stewardship (using, restoring, serving, keeping, entrusting).

Our ultimate purpose is to honour God as Creator in such a way that Christian environmental stewardship is part and parcel of everything we do. Our goal is to make tending the garden of creation in all its aspects an unquestioned and all-pervasive aspect of our service to each other, to our community, and to God's world. Awareness stands at the very beginning as the first of three components of creation stewardship.

Awareness means bringing things to our attention. In a time when so much calls for our attention – foreign affairs, local politics, jobs or traffic – the creation in its natural aspects does not even seem real to us. We might find that it seems real only on some of our travels, and even then it may be seriously obscured. We must consciously make ourselves aware of what is happening in God's creation.

Awareness involves seeing, naming, identifying, locating. It means taking off the blinkers provided by ourselves and society so that we not only see God's creation, but also want to name and know the names of the things we see. It means providing ourselves with enough peace and thoughtfulness to give ourselves the time and the will to identify a tree or mountain, bird or river. It means having the sense to enter the natural world intentionally in order to locate and find God's creatures that we sing about in the doxology, 'Praise God, all creatures here below.'

Awareness, however, is not an end in itself. From awareness comes appreciation; we cannot appreciate that of which we are unaware. At the very least, appreciation means tolerating that of which we are aware. We may tolerate spiders and hyenas, for example, and in so doing appreciate them. But beyond toleration, appreciation can also mean respect. We certainly respect a large bear, but we also can develop respect for a lowly worm as we learn of its critical importance to the rest of creation (including ourselves). Appreciation can build from toleration, to respect, and on to valuing. We know that God declares creation to be good, and we will find that God does so for good reason. As we become aware of the order of creation, we will find ourselves imaging God's valuing of the creatures. And this will build even further until much of what we discover we will even esteem and cherish. Thus, awareness will lead to appreciation.

Furthermore, appreciation does not end the matter, for appreciation leads to stewardship. At first, stewardship may mean the use of creation: perhaps our appreciation for a flower will lead us to put it in a vase to decorate our table. Stewardship, however, will bring us well beyond appropriate use to restoration of what has been abused in the past. The widespread lack of awareness and ignorance of creation and creation's integrity mean that we and many others have abused and degraded the environment unknowingly, and stewardship means that we will work to set things right again – to reconcile and redeem. We might even buy back something degraded to make it right again (see DeWitt 1998).

Beyond restoration, stewardship means serving. As we understand that God through creation is in so many ways serving our own lives, we will return this service with our own. This service will include keeping lovingly and caringly that which we hold in trust. And our service in creation will lead us to entrust others with what we have served, kept and restored.

Christian environmental stewardship – our loving care and keeping of creation – is a central, joyful, part of the human task. As communities of God's stewards – as the body of the one who made, sustains, and reconciles the world – our churches and our lives can be, and must be, vibrant testimonies to our Redeemer and Creator.

'Thou art worthy, O Lord, to receive glory and honour, and power: for thou hast created all things, and for thy will's sake they are, and have been created' (Rev. 4:11, Geneva Bible).

5
The *Declaration* under siege

Richard T. Wright

Richard T. Wright taught at Gordon College, Massachusetts, for thirty-three years following degrees from Rutgers and Harvard Universities. He is a marine microbiologist, well known for his widely used textbook Environmental Science *(7th edition, 2000) as well as his* Biology through the Eyes of Faith *(1989).*

There is a very active anti-environmental movement in the United States, rooted in free-enterprise ideology, and funded by industries like timber, real estate, mining, oil and gas which are dependent on exploiting natural resources and are often targeted by environmentalist critique. The highest achievement of this movement was the 'Contract with America' promoted by the Republican Party in the 1990s. A broad-based attack on existing environmental legislation, the Contract largely failed because of lack of public support. Nevertheless, a large element of the Republican Party has persisted in attempts to undermine environmental progress, and has succeeded in blocking the renewal of the Endangered Species Act and in frustrating any US action on the Kyoto Accord to curb greenhouse-gas emissions.

This is a conservative movement, politically and ideologically connected to the free-enterprise capitalism that has long been a dominant feature of the American scene. Oddly – at least to some – the movement has a great deal of support in some evangelical Christian circles. There is much sympathy among conservative Christians for the Republican Party – the 'religious Right' that has been flexing its political muscles in recent years. It should not be surprising, therefore, that when strong support for environmentalist ideals emerged from other conservative Christian sources, there was a reaction. *An Evangelical Declaration on the Care of Creation* presented a challenge to the Christian Right that had to be countered – and it was.

Before it was even made public, *World*, a Christian current-affairs weekly published in North Carolina, published a critique of the *Declaration* (Beisner 1993). Prior to this, *World* had already established a record of attacking environmentalists. In one issue, *World* compared the US Environmental Protection Agency with the Gestapo, claiming that regulations go 'far beyond minimal standards for good health. The social engineers of our government are absolutely committed to bigger government and national socialism' (Bomer 1993a). Environmentalists were pictured as deliberately putting people out of work by their involvement in the controversy over timber-harvesting and endangered species like the spotted owl (Bomer 1993b). So a critical approach to the *Declaration* was entirely consistent with *World*'s editorial policies.

World's feature article was entitled 'Are God's resources finite?' and subtitled 'A group of Christian leaders claim they are, but does the claim square with the evidence?' An introductory section of the article gives a brief account of the context of the *Declaration*, highlighting the creation of the National Religious Partnership for the Environment, and calls from Vice-President Gore and astronomer Carl Sagan for more involvement of religion in environmental issues. After identifying the drafters of the *Declaration*, *World* handed over the task of analysis to E. Calvin Beisner, an economist and lecturer at Covenant College (a Christian college in Tennessee), and also the author of (now) two books critical of environmentalist positions (Beisner 1990, 1997).

Beisner dismissed the *Declaration*'s call to work for godly, just, sustainable economies, and its call for responsible public policies embodying the principles of biblical stewardship, by declaring them so vague as to prohibit specific criticisms. He then attacked the pessimistic view the *Declaration* takes of the state of the environment. He focused on the seven degradations of creation listed in the *Declaration* (see pp. 61–62 in this book), deploring the lack of specificity in the account of degradations, as this makes it harder to criticize them. Nevertheless, he goes on record to counter each one of them with claims to the contrary.

Land degradation? How could this be true if *per capita* grain production continues to rise steeply, for every major region of the world and regardless of income level? (Apparently Beisner was unaware that *per capita* grain production peaked in 1984 and has been on a decline ever since; and that sub-Saharan Africa has experienced a decline since 1972.)

Deforestation? Long-term trends do not support this claim. According to the UN Food and Agricultural Organization (FAO), total world forested area was higher by the mid-1980s than at the end of the 1940s, and is rising. (Actually, the FAO has recently documented a net loss of 180 million hectares of forest between 1980 and 1995, or 12 million hectares per year.)

Species extinction? Since the *Declaration* doesn't provide any rate or trend, Beisner turned to DeWitt's published work to refute DeWitt's claims that three species are extinguished daily (1,100 per year, therefore). At most, Beisner states, the rate is similar to what it has been for thousands of years of human history – perhaps one per century. (This claim is so patently wrong that it needs no rejoinder.)

Water degradation? Beisner says, 'There simply is no evidence that freshwater resources are significantly endangered.' (Contaminated water accounts for 7% of all deaths and disease worldwide, according to the World Health Organization.)

Global toxification? Referring to pollution by DDT or similar chemicals, Beisner states that 'no data support major worldwide damage done by such chemicals'. In fact, according to one biochemist Beisner cites, our real problem is the natural pesticides produced by plants.

Alteration of atmosphere? Quoting Beisner, 'Hard data do not support the claim either that global warming and long-term ozone depletion are occurring or that there is a significant correlation between human activity and global temperature and ozone trends.' (More recently, Beisner and *World* have made global warming a major concern as they have criticized the Kyoto Accord forged in December 1997. Beisner [1998] claims in an article entitled 'Putting Kyoto on ice' that the Accord would slow economic progress in the Third World to such a degree that 4 billion persons could suffer and die prematurely!)

Human and cultural degradation? Beisner isn't sure what this means, so he cites the rise in average life expectancy that indicates how much better things are for people the world over. (With 840 million malnourished or undernourished, and 1.3 billion living in abject poverty, it would seem a bit cavalier to deny that there isn't something wrong here.)

So much for a degraded creation. Beisner says that the *Declaration* portrays a view of the environment that is simply not accurate. Even worse, it mimics the claims of crisis in the 'secular environmental movement' without checking their accuracy. However, Beisner goes on to affirm a few good things about the *Declaration*. It does address the link between poverty and environmental degradation (just in case it is degraded), and supports free economies that create the wealth necessary to protect and restore the environment. The *Declaration* rightly calls Christians to stewardship, even though it doesn't say much about what that is. And it warns against turning to non-Christian religions and against confusing the creation with the Creator.

But there's an even greater source of weakness in the document, says Beisner, and that is theological. Although the Earth is the Lord's (Ps. 24:1), it has been given over to humans for ownership (Ps. 115:16), and thus stewardship can also involve true ownership by people. And Beisner faults the authors for failing to distinguish the garden of Eden from the wilderness outside. In fact, Adam and Eve were instructed to guard and cultivate the garden from the surrounding wilderness. And because the Earth was eventually placed under a curse because of the fall, 'nature transformed by wise, godly human stewardship' is superior to nature untouched by human hands. Beisner goes on to celebrate the human creativity that has led to modern civilization and the vast creation of wealth. Indeed, the very idea that 'we are pressing against the finite limits God has set for creation', as the *Declaration* puts it, ignores the realities of human creativity and its ability to expand the limits of resources indefinitely. People are not a burden to the Earth; they are a blessing. What we are doing, in fact, is to transform 'the cursed earth – the wilderness – into a garden', according to Beisner. (Surely this begs the question of how the human sinfulness that led to the fall could be expected to subside so that our 'transformations' would result in improvements of raw nature. The *Declaration* doesn't deny human creativity – it calls for more of it, to be applied to healing creation and to living out the biblical principles listed in the last section [pp. 19–22], and to working for public policies that embody stewardship.)

World's attack on the *Declaration* drew a quick response from some of its authors. Gordon Aeschliman, then editor of *Prism*, a journal published by Evangelicals for Social Action (ESA), took *World* to task for affirming that there is no substantial environmental problem in the world today. Says

Aeschliman (1994), 'We don't know what world they are referring to.' He goes on to document Beisner's assertions of good things getting better, and states that 'Beisner hasn't done his homework on God's earth'.

More important, however, says Aeschliman, is the theological problem reflected by Beisner's view of the fall. 'It is precisely the impact of the Fall that calls the church to take its mandates seriously.' Is human creativity leading to fidelity and covenant-keeping in solving the problems of marriages and the family that are the outcome of the fall? Will urban youth express their creativity and walk away from the stresses of drugs and violence? Can we hope that oppressive governments will in time be creative and forgo their sinful practices? Aeschliman calls on *World* to pull its head out of the sand and join in affirming the Christian stewardship that is called for in the *Declaration* – or at least to join in the dialogue of Christian stewardship and what it means.

To their credit, *World* then gave ESA's President Ron Sider, another of the authors of the *Declaration*, an opportunity to respond to the *World* critique (Sider 1994; see also pp. 43–49 in this volume). Sider immediately faults Beisner for making some wrong assumptions in his criticisms of the *Declaration*. For example, Beisner assumed that the *Declaration*'s call for 'sustainable economies' excluded the economies of the developed countries, since environmentalist ideology dismisses them as inherently unsustainable. Not so, says Sider. Those economies need to be addressed specifically in areas of energy use, recycling and pollution. Like Aeschliman, Sider especially takes Beisner to task on his overly optimistic assessment of human progress despite the effects of the fall. 'Has an overly optimistic postmillennialism led him to overlook the way economic injustice, greed, and narcissistic individualism trample the poor and mar the environment?' Finally, Sider cites Beisner's lack of understanding of the scientific consensus on the environment, in particular the question of species extinctions. Sider closed by calling on *World*'s editors and readers to take a good look at the scientific data and to follow the truth wherever it might lead.

In the same issue, Beisner gave a short rejoinder to Sider, rebutted Sider's criticism, and repeated his criticism of the *Declaration*. At that point, the exchange ended, the opponents apparently convinced that there was little point in trying to change anyone's mind on the matter.

Is there a lesson in this exchange of editorial shots? I think so. Above all, the exchange clearly documented a rift in evangelical Christianity in the US that continues to this day. Many Christians are still opposed to major elements of the environmental agenda. The opposition to any US support of United Nations family-planning programmes is a case in point. Although the message and ethic of stewardship are spreading throughout the secular and even academic arenas, they have not been wholeheartedly embraced by all evangelical Christians. Why is this so? The answer seems to be that Christian anti-environmentalism is a direct consequence of political commitments (Wright 1995). The theological considerations are of secondary importance, although they may be used to justify the politically motivated opposition. People who are conservative in their religious views are very often conservative in their politics. They are often reluctant to side with groups that are perceived as being more liberal, usually pro-Democratic Party, as the environmental organizations often are. Worse, many environmental activists also support pro-choice views on abortion, multiculturalism, secular humanism, New Age religions and radical feminism. Who wants to keep company with such people? It becomes too easy to lump environmental concerns with a lot of this less desirable baggage, and oppose it all.

What to do, then? There are such powerful worldview elements at work that it is very difficult to convince people of their short-sighted dismissal of the kinds of concerns laid out in the *Declaration*. There is still a very active anti-environmentalism alive in the United States, and many Christians have bought into it. In my view, the hope lies in the future generation of Christians, who will be far less able to ignore the seven degradations of creation as they worsen. The message of 'creation care' is spreading, and it is hard to deny. I am hopeful that its unassailable truthfulness will eventually bring about a greater consensus in Christendom. The Lord knows we need it.

Part III
Commentary

The factors that led to the *Declaration* have been described in the preceding contributions. However, it should not be thought that the group responsible for the document (pp. 50–51) assumed that they possessed all wisdom. A draft version was circulated to Christian leaders in the USA for approval and criticism, and revisions were made before the *Declaration* was issued in 1994.

Despite the adjustments made to the original text, it is interesting that the more thoughtful comments directed against the original draft are points that resurface in the comments that follow: the relationship of the Creator to his creation; the involvement of all three persons of the Trinity; the role of humans in dealing with creation (stewardship, repairing and renewing, worshipping the Creator along with the non-human creation); the interpretation of particular scriptures; the link between environmental action, religious (or moral) motivation, and Christian commitment; and the effects of the fall and God's curse upon the ground.

There were and probably always will be Christians who regard the *Declaration* as misguided or irrelevant (see Wright's discussion of the attacks by Calvin Beisner, pp. 75–76, and Drake Emmerich's description of the situation on Tangier Island, pp. 148–149), but its overall content seems to have met general acceptance, as witnessed the several hundred church leaders who have formally endorsed its message. The test, of course, comes not from merely agreeing with a text, but in actions that follow such agreement. That is where the fourteen essays in this section are pertinent, because they represent fourteen independent and considered responses to the coherence and persuasiveness of the *Declaration*.

My invitations to comment went to theologians and environmental practitioners. I asked the same thing from all of them: to comment critically or positively about all or any part of the *Declaration*. With such unspecific guidance, I expected that there might be considerable overlap between contributions; I feared that there would be a significant editorial task in welding together the individual comments. In fact, there proved to be singularly little overlap or disagreement between individual essays. Through no effort on my behalf, the commentators have produced a set of positive and complementary approaches to the care of creation. As a consequence, I have done little to remove the fairly small amount of repetition in different essays.

This does not mean that everyone who has contributed agrees with the *Declaration* in its entirety, but all the comments deal with emphases rather than major dissension; no contributor wants to amend or add to the *Declaration* in any significant way.

The first five essays in this section are by major theologians. Alister McGrath sets the scene by pointing out and reviewing some of the studies on creation care by both theologians and scientists, particularly during the 1990s. Oliver O'Donovan and Richard Bauckham concentrate on the rich vein of scriptural admonitions to wonder and rejoice at God's creation work, which is a far stronger emphasis than the commands and mandate to exercise stewardship. Howard Marshall underpins our responsibility to exercise creation care, as part of God's divine pattern for the world – and for us. Jürgen Moltmann links the maturing calls of various church bodies to the need for specific responses: a cosmic spirituality as God's Spirit shapes, supports and strengthens us; a wider understanding of God's covenant with his creation; and an ecological as well as a social obedience to the Sabbath commands.

The theologians are followed by three scientists. Ghillean Prance points out the increasing recognition from all quarters that environmental problems will begin to be dealt with successfully only when we are morally committed to responding to them. This is not novel: White concluded his 1967 paper with the words, 'Since the roots of our trouble are so largely religious, the remedy must also be essentially religious, whether we call it that or not' (p. 42); Francis Schaeffer (1972) believed the same. Howard Van Till directs his remarks mainly to Christians, arguing that creation care is a divine obligation laid on all of us, and not one which can be avoided on the grounds that our present world is merely a temporary phase in God's dispensation, and that we often misname creation as 'nature' or 'environment' and hence draw attention away from the Creator. John Houghton complements Van Till's paper, reminding us of the global damage that we are causing. Like Prance, he identifies the need for moral leadership, with the implication that failure in this realm is disobedience to God.

The next four papers are by people who have faced the uncomfortable but exciting challenge to work out the *Declaration* principles in practice: Peter Harris of A Rocha, who has established first one and then several field study centres and has had to fight against traditional attitudes because of reinterpreting old texts in more rigorous ways; Stephen Rand of Tearfund, who shows that loving one's neighbour is terribly misapplied if it is taken as merely loving his or her soul; Susan Drake Emmerich, who found exactly the same thing in her life in a fishing community where the catches were in apparent inexorable decline; and John Guillebaud, who concentrates on a single paragraph of the *Declaration* to remind us of the links between the numbers of people, their poverty (or affluence) and their impacts on the environment.

Finally, there are two contributions from what may be called 'practical theologians'. Ron Elsdon highlights the need to develop a coherent eschatology of this world, particularly in the light of its sinful nature; and Michael Northcott develops a parallel theme of false worship and the inevitable problems thus wrought on a creation as God's (or natural) laws are ignored.

6

The stewardship of the creation: an evangelical affirmation

Alister E. McGrath

Alister E. McGrath is Principal of Wycliffe Hall, Oxford, and Professor of Historical Theology at Oxford University. He has a doctorate in molecular biology from Oxford and has studied theology at both Oxford and Cambridge Universities. He has written widely on the Reformation, and on the relationships between science and Christianity (see, for example, The Foundations of Dialogue in Science and Religion, *1998).*

The biblical notion of creation is enormously rich and complex, and offers a number of insights of determinative importance in relation to the issue of the care of creation as summarized in the *Declaration* (see, for example, Gilkey 1959, Napier 1962, Thompson 1971, Brooke 1987, van Bavel 1990, Leslie 1993, Lohfink 1994, Oelschlaeger 1994, May 1995, Hartlieb 1996 and Bouma-Prediger 1997). The following points emerge from any responsible attempt to take seriously the biblical insights concerning creation:

1. The natural order, including humanity, is the result of God's act of creation, and is affirmed to be God's possession.
2. Humanity is distinguished from the remainder of creation in terms of being created in the 'image of God'.
3. Humanity is charged with the tending of creation (as Adam was entrusted with the care of Eden), in the full knowledge that this creation is the cherished possession of God.

4. There is thus no theological ground for asserting that humanity has the 'right' to do what it pleases with the natural order. The creation is God's, and has been entrusted to humanity, who is to act as its steward, not its exploiter.

It is important to notice how the creation narratives can function as the basis of a rigorously grounded approach to ecology (see, for example, Oelschlaeger 1994). This has been set out in a particularly attractive manner in a recent study by Calvin B. DeWitt. He has argued that four fundamental ecological principles can readily be discerned within the biblical narratives (DeWitt 1995; see also DeWitt's article on pp. 60–73 above):

1. The 'Earth-keeping principle': just as the Creator keeps and sustains humanity, so humanity must keep and sustain the Creator's creation.
2. The 'Sabbath principle': the creation must be allowed to recover from human use of its resources.
3. The 'fruitfulness principle': the fecundity of the creation is to be enjoyed, not destroyed.
4. The 'fulfilment and limits principle': there are limits set to humanity's role within creation, with boundaries set in place which must be respected.

In making such basic points, it must be pointed out that the more sceptical sections of the scientific community have generally failed to note them. Such sceptics persist in portraying Christianity as lending some kind of ideological sanction to the unprincipled and unlimited exploitation of the environment. In 1967, Lynn White published an influential article in which he asserted that Christianity was to blame for the emerging ecological crisis on account of its using the concept of the 'image of God', found in the Genesis creation account (Gen. 1:26–27), as a pretext for justifying human exploitation of the world's resources (White 1967; see pp. 31–42). Genesis, he argued, legitimated the notion of human domination over the creation, hence leading to its exploitation. Despite (or perhaps on account of) its historical and theological superficiality, White's paper had a profound impact on the shaping of popular scientific attitudes towards Christianity in particular, and religion in general.

With the passage of time, a more sanguine estimation of White's argument has gained the ascendancy (summarized in Whitney 1993). The argument is now recognized to be seriously flawed. A closer reading of the Genesis text showed that such themes as 'humanity as the steward of creation' and 'humanity as the partner of God' are indicated by the text, rather than that of 'humanity as the lord of creation' (Barr 1968; Preuss 1995: 2:114–117). Furthermore, a careful study of the reception of this text within the Judeo-Christian tradition makes it clear that White's interpretation simply cannot be sustained (Cohen 1989). Far from being the enemy of ecology, the doctrine of creation affirms the importance of human responsibility towards the environment. In a widely read study, the distinguished Canadian writer Douglas John Hall stressed that the biblical concept of 'domination' was to be understood specifically in terms of 'stewardship' (Hall 1986). To put it simply: creation is not the possession of humanity; it is something which is to be seen as entrusted to humanity, who is responsible for its safekeeping and tending (Nash 1991; Cobb 1992).

A further contribution has been made by the German theologian Jürgen Moltmann, noted for his concern to ensure the theologically rigorous application of Christian theology to social, political and environmental issues (Bauckham 1993; Bouma-Prediger 1997). For example, in *God in Creation*, Moltmann (1985) argues that the exploitation of the world reflects the rise of technology, and seems to have little to do with specifically Christian teachings. Furthermore, he stresses the manner in which God can be said to indwell the creation through the Holy Spirit, so that the pillage of creation becomes an assault on God. On the basis of this analysis, Moltmann is able to offer a rigorously Trinitarian defence of a distinctively Christian ecological ethic (see pp. 107–113). This point merits further discussion.

A fundamental theme of modernism – a term which is usually taken to refer to the cultural mood which began to emerge towards the opening of the twentieth century – is its desire to control, perhaps seen at its clearest in the Nietzschean theme of 'will-to-power'. Humanity needs only the will to achieve autonomous self-definition; it need not accept what has been given to it, whether in nature or tradition. In principle, all can be mastered and controlled. This desire for liberation was often linked with the mythical figure of Prometheus, who came to be seen as a symbol of liberation in European literature (Trousson 1976; Lewis 1992; Wilson 1998). The rise of technology was seen as paralleling Prometheus' theft of fire from the gods. Limits were removed. Prometheus was now unbound, and humanity was poised to enter a new era of autonomy and progress. The rise of technology was seen as a tool to allow humanity to control its environment, without the need to respect natural limitations.

If anything can be identified as the enemy of those who care for creation, it is the ruthless human tendency to exploit and to refuse to accept that limits have been set for human behaviour and activity. For the evangelical, the fundamental element of original sin (as described in Genesis 3) is a desire to be able to be like God, and be set free from all the restraints of creatureliness. This resolute refusal to accept a properly constituted place within creation can easily be seen to be linked with the development of tools by which humanity is no longer obligated to operate under any form of moral or physical restraint. White's thesis is right in one sense: Genesis does indeed contain the key to human exploitation of the world. Yet that key lies in the fall of humanity and the refusal to acknowledge the limits of human competence and authority. If we are to regain John Milton's 'enormous bliss' of Eden, it must be through recognizing our limitations as God's creatures, and more specifically our obligations to tend and care for God's good creation. That means at least a rediscovery of Genesis, and certainly a more attentive reading than that offered by Lynn White.

7

'Where were you ...?'

Oliver M. T. O'Donovan

Oliver M. T. O'Donovan is Regius Professor of Moral and Pastoral Theology in the University of Oxford, a Canon of Christchurch Cathedral, Oxford, and a significant contributor to evangelical understanding of moral order. He is the author of Resurrection and Moral Order *(1986) and* The Desire of the Nations *(1996), and other works.*

'*Where were you ... ?*' (Job 38:4). That scornful question hurled by the Creator at the complaining self-pity of one of nature's victims is meant to drag us out of our complacency. Job must learn not to think of nature only in relation to his own wants, but to see the irrelevance of those wants to the vast universe of nature. He is to be humbled by a pageant of natural phenomena, glorious in its sheer observational detail: oceanology, geology, meteorology, astronomy and, of course, lots of unforgettable animal ethology. The scientific wonder of the ancient world, more unforced than our own, makes this proud specimen of our race feel very small. He has no claim to a stable and well-balanced ecosystem in the face of a nature so diverse in its teleologies, so indifferent to human concerns. When the Creator made the ostrich so forgetful as to leave her eggs on the desert floor for any passing foot to trample on, and so powerful in her wingspan as to outstrip a mounted hunter, it was not for Job's entertainment that he did it.

In the book of Job, God speaks with nature's voice, because nature excites a palpable sense of our human contingency and teaches us to worship. Our problem today, which is also the *cause* of our problems in the more specific sense, is that our awe has given way to an exploitative and managerial approach to nature. There are many – scientists and non-scientists alike – who would like to call us back to awe; but that is a path that seems no longer open to us. When the greatest of the beasts before whom our ancestors shrank in terror is in danger of extinction, when the very biodiversity of the planet seems to depend on the implementation of a political treaty, the only thing to be in awe of is the dizzying power of human culture. The titles roll off the press: *In Defence of Creation, Can Creation be Saved?* and so on. They merely underline the changed relation which exists between us and the natural world. It seems that the damage is done. We are locked in to managing nature as if it was a pathetic dependant upon our kind consideration and foresight. Like it or not, the fate of the ostrich depends on the entertainment she affords to Job's children on their television screens – before nine o'clock, of course, because nature is quite unfrightening, even for small children.

The awareness of this transformation of attitude, to which *An Evangelical Declaration on the Care of Creation* makes a contribution, is a phenomenon of our time. The sources of the change lie not in our own day, but far back in the roots of our modern civilization. It is reasonable to trace it to new ontological configurations in the fourteenth century, which began to dissolve 'real kinds' into discrete individuated phenomena; to new epistemological configurations in the sixteenth century, which taught us to doubt the evidence of our senses and to 'put nature to the torture' (in Bacon's famous phrase) to tell us the truth; and to new philosophies of history in the seventeenth and eighteenth centuries which looked for a story of progress won by human mastery and manipulation. It is impossible, however, for the *Declaration* to say very much about this, because there is too much to be said. It is therefore wisely content to note the suggestion that a 'spiritual crisis' lies at the root of the problem.

It is impossible not to be grateful for an attempt to place our awareness of the ecological crisis in the context of the Christian faith, and to articulate, in however general terms, some programmes for a responsible pattern of life. Those programmes, which are broadly enough conceived to include celebration, care and study, as well as personal virtues of 'humility, forbearance, self-restraint and frugality', seem, nevertheless, to leave some questions open. Does the call for 'just, free economies' encompass the biblical mandate to *share* our goods? And do the virtues of 'forbearance' and 'restraint' extend to research and technology, as well as to consumption? Absent from the list of concerns, it seems, is the human manipulation of *human* nature, as practised, for example, in genetic technology.

Yet, on reading the *Declaration*, we may be rather more struck by a bleakness of tone: vain regrets, guilt by association, determined resolutions of the will. Why, we may wonder, is it called an *evangelical* declaration? What is the Good News in which it calls us to put our trust? A wise theologian said that what we need is not belief in Creation, but belief in the Creator. I am not at all sure how well the *Declaration* succeeds in pointing us beyond our human perspectives to the God who encompasses us, and all our possible environments, in his judgment and care. One evangelical phrase is missing: 'Do not be anxious!'

It might, for example, have evoked our memory of *God as the beginning of our beginnings*, who launched created nature and our humanity upon their improbable cohabitation. Cosmic beginnings remain intensely fascinating to our generation. I have heard it said that prehistory – the dinosaurs and earlier – is still the strongest argument in the contemporary mind for disbelieving in the existence of God. I suspect that may be true, for it is certainly the strongest argument for disbelieving in the existence of human beings. To gaze seriously at those beginnings is to experience a dizzying terror at the utter improbability of our own race; and when human beings are improbable, the God who risked himself in covenant with human beings is improbable as well. But the strongest argument against belief in the existence of God may be the strongest reason for faith in God. For we ourselves, after all, are that most improbable of all outcomes of evolution: the human race.

More might have been said about the *covenant of God with creation*, and of his faithfulness, which is greater than our faithlessness. While the authors speak of God's purposes of healing, I find it particularly disappointing that they find no place to affirm that the Word-become-flesh is the ground of our hope. That God himself has assumed our human nature; and that the Word which gave rise to the universe has become the partner of our threatened humanity: those affirmations imply a degree of peril which no depiction of environmental degradation can quite match up to; and they imply a hope which no programme for 'humility, forbearance, self-restraint and frugality' can quite extend to us.

It is, perhaps, symptomatic that the *Declaration* can find no English word to refer to that *species* of creaturely flesh which the Word of God became; the same species as that to which the 'we' of the *Declaration*, as well as all who will read it and attend to it, belong. The phrase 'men, women and children' is no substitute for speaking of 'man', 'mankind', 'humankind', 'humanity', 'the human race', or whatever form of reference to our kind that may commend itself to socially aware susceptibilities. A failure of nerve in speaking of *that* highest work of God's creation, *that* supreme object of the divine compassion, *that* elect partner of God's divinity in the person of Christ, suggests a failure of nerve about the meaning of the incarnation itself.

More might have been said, finally, about the effective and terrible *judgment of God* in nature. It is bad faith, of course, to make fashionable talk (which the authors of the *Declaration* rightly avoid) about 'defending creation'. It is not creation as such, but our own tight little ecosystem that is on the line. Nature, we know, could shrug it off and develop a thousand other ecosystems quite as easily as a sleeper turning in bed and rearranging the blanket. We can be fairly certain that there will then be a universe fit for viruses to thrive in. The question is whether, among the infinite possibilities for nature's regeneration, there would exist even one which counts us human beings in.

Perhaps, after all, we are not so far removed from the terror which the Old Testament writers experienced in contemplating nature – if only we look in the right direction. As the psalmist lay in his bed at night he heard the cry of lions on the hunt: 'the lions roar for their prey ...' (Ps. 104:21). He knew that in the daytime, when they were sleeping off their kill, the country would be safe for men to go abroad and do their work – but only, as it were, protected within their fragile reserve. Humankind must study to learn its place, lest the slender protections which surrounded it be swept away. The modern North American on the beach in summer, pulling his baseball cap nervously over his eyes and lathering every inch of exposed skin with costly sunblock cream (which may, for all he knows, induce the very cancers he is hoping to ward off) has heard a different sound, but the message is the same. If the lions are tame now, thanks to big-game hunters and television crews, something as pleasant and friendly as the summer sun is suddenly wild and dangerous. Nature, like the wind, has swung to a different quarter; she blows unfamiliarly, but strongly.

Are we prepared to hear, through her inhospitable roar, the voice of the Creator, warning and counselling us about our ways? If we are in too great a hurry to accept the responsibility for managing things better, we may never hear the question that he is putting to us. Let our first response, like Job's, be to lay our hands on our mouths.

8
Commitment to creation

I. Howard Marshall

I. Howard Marshall was Professor of New Testament Exegesis at the University of Aberdeen from 1979 to 1999. He is a Methodist minister. Howard Marshall has been a major contributor to evangelical New Testament scholarship and has published a number of important commentaries.

One of the things that inhibits some Christians from assenting whole-heartedly to the kind of declaration which is the subject of this book is the lack of any clear commands in the New Testament to believers to engage in such matters. There is a feeling that we have plenty to do in fulfilling the commands that *are* there, and that there is a danger of concentrating on secondary matters and ignoring more central ones if we engage in areas that appear to be peripheral to the concerns of the first Christians. For many Christians there is no doubt that the New Testament is primarily concerned with spiritual welfare, and all that it says about the renewal of creation and the resurrection of the body does little to shift the focus for them. They have a good case. Even in matters of church order it is difficult to get some Christian groups to go beyond following the explicit instructions in the New Testament (although in fact they cannot help being influenced by later traditions); Calvin was able to smuggle a good deal of practice in under the general rubric of 'do all things decently and in order', and to some extent people are prepared to go along the line of 'whatever is not expressly forbidden in Scripture and is not contrary to its spirit is permissible'. Nevertheless, church order on the whole remains pretty conservative and there isn't a lot of innovation around.

In the case of care for the creation, it is perhaps not surprising that there is little explicit teaching about it in the Bible in general and in the New Testament in particular. On the one hand, the biblical writers were concerned primarily with the relationship between God and human beings, and this concern naturally dwarfs all others. On the other hand, there was a general unawareness of many problems that have come to the consciousness of people today. To be sure, we should not despise or look down on ancient people and congratulate ourselves for our fuller insights; we have only to think of the things that were tolerated even within the last two hundred years (the persistence of slavery, the inhuman conditions under which children worked, and the lack of rights for women), and also of the things that actually happen in so-called civilized nations today (the genocide in parts of Europe, and the wanton killing of innocent people to secure political advantages nearer home). Nevertheless, it remains true that the contemporary awareness of social problems and of the problems of the environment was, by and large, not part of ancient thinking. After all, the environment hardly constituted a problem, in view of the comparative smallness of the world's population at that time and of its limited capacity to plunder or destroy nature. In no way could there have been a consciousness of the problem that we now have, which is so largely the result of the behaviour of sinful people.

It is not surprising, then, that there is not much in the Bible, especially in the New Testament, about these things. And already it will be obvious that this silence is not in itself a reason for us to be similarly unconcerned; the silence is partly at least because the world then was different.

In order to take a step forward in discussing our immediate problem – care for the world – it may be useful to consider the analogy of social concern and see how it is treated in Scripture. Some people today may justify their lack of involvement in politics, both national and local, and in the social problems of the world, by pointing to the way in which the early Christians were so busy with evangelism and the upbuilding of the church that they had little, if any, time for such secondary matters. Their responsibility was to treat their immediate family and neighbours in a Christian way, and there their responsibility ended.

It is a proper response to people who adopt this line of argument that they have not taken the example of God's people in the Old Testament with sufficient seriousness. Here a very great deal of space is devoted to the words and actions of the prophets, who were prepared to intervene powerfully in the affairs of state, to condemn rulers for making dubious alliances with foreign countries, to attack injustice to the poor, and to champion the cause of widows and orphans (the most vulnerable members of society). Elijah attacks King Ahab to his face over his acquisition of Naboth's vineyard; Amos inveighs against cruelty in time of war; Isaiah condemns the Assyrians for their cruel oppression of Israel that went far beyond reasonable limits. Samuel was a constant thorn in the side of King Saul. There is no shortage in the Old Testament of people called by God to deliver a divine commentary on the shortcomings of government and armies and to protest against local injustices and shady dealings.

Since the Old Testament is part of Christian Scripture, here we have an irrefutable example of God's people being involved in the political and social issues of the day. We can easily understand why there is a lack of similar involvement in the New Testament, when the Christian church was still at the stage of birth and infancy, and when it was not yet in a position to influence politics and social affairs. But with the growth of the church such activity becomes possible and mandatory. We are reminded that 'everything that was written in the past was written to teach us' (Rom. 15:4), and the example of the prophets is there to be followed.

Must we now not say also that, even if there is little apparent concern for creation in the New Testament and not much more in the Old, there can still in the same way be an obligation upon us to show such concern? The case for social and political protest by Christians is based on the example of God's people in the Old Testament, even though there is little specific instruction on this matter in the New Testament. Similarly, the case for concern for the world rests on theological principles and some commands which must be articulated in action.

First, the world is the creation of God who made it and took delight in it, and it is entirely reasonable that he should expect the special creatures made in his image and likeness to share this concern. If God's people are to be like their God, this must include his love and care for the world.

Second, Adam and Eve were specifically commanded to work in the garden and take care of it. The story of Adam and Eve is paradigmatic of God's intention for humanity, and the fact of the fall and their expulsion from the garden does not indicate that this command has been abrogated.

Third, prophecies of the future include the vision of a renewed and fruitful Earth, and indicate that this is God's original purpose and intention for the world; his people should share his vision.

Fourth, the fact that human beings have a responsibility to love one another carries the implication that they must tend the world so that it can continue to provide space and food for people to live; even if the world were there simply for human benefit, there is still a responsible use of its resources so that these are maintained for the benefit of all people.

Fifth, God's people are expected to live wisely (Proverbs!) with renewed minds, and they must surely use their God-given intelligence and insight in doing their work responsibly in an enlightened manner. It is clear enough that the problems which beset the environment today are due to two main causes: one is human greed and violence, but the other is human ignorance as to the best policies to adopt for the benefit of the world and its inhabitants. Christians need both love and knowledge in order to exercise their stewardship of creation.

What is being argued here is that, just as the responsibility of Christians for political and social involvement rests not on direct command but on an application of the examples found in Scripture (especially the Old Testament), so the responsibility for care for the world rests not on direct command but on application of the principles which are to be found in Scripture. Most Christians have in fact come to see that they have a political and social responsibility. This varies in degree. Not all of God's people were called to be prophets capable of challenging rulers, but the people as a whole were meant to back up the prophets so that the latter spoke in the name of God and his people against oppression and injustice. Equally, while we all have a responsibility for the care of the world, not all Christians today are called to take an active initiative in environmental issues, but there will be some for whom it is a special responsibility.

It is sometimes suggested that the political and social analogy doesn't take us beyond the limit of protest against wrong; it doesn't require us to get involved positively in political leadership and social work. Again the analogy of the people of God in the Old Testament is a powerful antidote to such evasion. What God wanted for his people was godly rulers, and it is well known that in the books of Kings the rulers are approved or condemned according as they walked or didn't walk in the ways of the Lord. There were prophets and there were judges who were national leaders (like Gideon and Samuel). Local rulers were expected to be God-fearing and to practise justice and compassion. The alternative was ungodly rulers, and these are uniformly condemned. So godly people were expected to rule. In the New Testament we hear of some mighty and some noble being converted, and there is nothing to suggest that upon conversion they gave up their imperial or civil roles. They remained in the situation in which God had called them. God still needs his people in positions of responsibility and government.

Equally, we may say, God needs his people to take the lead in care for the world and its peoples. Who else is going to act with love, justice, wisdom and knowledge, if it is not the people who love and serve him? (This is not to say that non-Christians are entirely lacking in such qualities; indeed, they may often show more of them than some Christians do.) We agree that some Christians can feel called of God to be physicians and surgeons. Neither of these is a profession which is to the forefront in Scripture, and certainly the idea of divine calling to take them would be hard to document. Why, then, should Christians not equally feel called of God to responsibility for the world of nature?

All this has been argument on a very simple level to show to people who follow the commands in Scripture that there can be implicit commands as well as explicit ones, and that there can be areas of concern which are only dimly perceived in Scripture which can take on a surprising prominence today and lay urgent responsibilities upon us. The fact that the New Testament has so comparatively little to say about care for the world should not blind us to the responsibilities that arise when we look at Scripture as a whole and recognize the theological principles that are latent in it and the corresponding obligations.

Living a responsible Christian life today is a far more complicated matter than it was in the first century. It is not too great an exaggeration to say that whatever happens across the globe has implications for each of us. Christians increasingly find that they have to know about a vast range of peoples and problems in the world, and they suffer from the explosion of knowledge. Therefore, it would seem appropriate that we identify the two or three issues on which we can concentrate our attention, instead of simply trying to be well informed about everything that is going on. But these issues should include not only the worldwide mission of the church and our responsibilities as Christian members of the local and national community, but also the problems of the world of nature. And all of them are issues which we take up in faith and in hope, knowing that the purpose of God, which he will fulfil, is the renewal of heaven and Earth, as well as of the people whom he created to inhabit the world.

9

Stewardship and relationship

Richard Bauckham

Richard Bauckham is Professor of Theology in the Divinity School of the University of St Andrews, Scotland. He read history at Clare College, Cambridge, and was a Fellow of St John's College. He later taught theology for one year at the University of Leeds, and for fifteen years at the University of Manchester, where he was Lecturer, then Reader, in the History of Christian Thought, before moving to St Andrews in 1992. A Fellow of the British Academy, he is a member of the Doctrine Commission of the Church of England and of the Doctrine Committee of the Scottish Episcopal Church, and he has published widely in theology and biblical studies.

I welcome the *Declaration* and very much hope it will serve to focus Christian concern and action for the care of creation. I offer some comments here especially on the notion of 'stewardship of creation', and hope to show that further reflection on this notion is needed to sharpen and to strengthen the aims of the *Declaration*.

Stewardship is the main image the *Declaration* employs to describe the proper human relationship to the rest of creation. Not a term often encountered in everyday modern usage, 'stewardship' has a biblical and Christian ring to it, which no doubt helps to commend it to us. But it is not a term the Bible itself uses of the human relationship to the rest of creation, nor was it used in this way by the Fathers, the medieval theologians or the Reformers. Such a use of the term stems only, so far as I know, from the seventeenth century (p. 101). It is worth acquainting ourselves with the circumstances in which it came into use. We cannot respond adequately to the crisis in the human relationship to the rest of creation which we now face, unless we understand how we have got to where we are. Our concepts, theological or otherwise, carry with them the history of modern humanity's great and disastrous project of conquering nature and remaking it to our own design.

The notion of humans as stewards of creation was intended, as the *Declaration* certainly also intends it, as an interpretation of the human 'dominion' over other creatures of which Genesis (1:26–28) speaks. (Surprisingly, the *Declaration* itself makes no explicit reference to Genesis 1:26–28, but it evidently presupposes some of the long history of Christian reflection on this text.) But stewardship was not the way the Genesis 'dominion' had most often been understood in the Christian theological tradition up to the seventeenth century. From the Fathers onwards, most Christian thinkers had interpreted the human dominion over creation with the aid of the idea, drawn from Greek philosophical rather than biblical sources, that the rest of creation exists for human benefit. The dominion was understood as the right to make use of all creatures for human ends. This is why many contemporary critics, following an extraordinarily influential essay published in 1967 by the medievalist Lynn White (see pp. 31–42), have seen in this Christian tradition the ideological source of the exploitative domination of nature, which in the modern period has produced the contemporary ecological crisis. However, it is important to notice that, before the early modern period, there was no sense of the dominion as an obligation to extend human mastery over nature, still less of the idea that nature is open to radical reshaping by human creativity. The dominion was understood in a static way, authorizing the rather limited use of their environment that humans then made. Moreover, the view that the world exists for human benefit was at least balanced by the more fundamental doctrine of creation: that humans are creatures of God alongside other creatures.

The modern project of technological domination of nature has its ideological roots, not in the Christian theological tradition itself, but in the way it was modified in Italian Renaissance humanism and by the English philosopher Francis Bacon. In the former, human dominion over the world was understood as a kind of divine sovereignty and creative freedom, such that humans have both the ability and the right to refashion nature as they choose. Any sense of humanity's creaturely limitations within God's creation was lost in the limitless aspiration to master and to create. The

Renaissance provided the vision which has inspired the modern project of dominating nature, while Francis Bacon turned the Genesis notion of dominion into a programme of scientific and technological enterprise, in which scientific mastery of nature's laws was to be the means of subjecting nature entirely to human use and benefit. This Baconian programme became the ideology which has inspired and governed scientific research and technological innovation down to the twentieth century. When we now castigate the destruction to which it has led, we should remember that it was inspired by high ideals (as are many of those who still accept it). It was a humanitarian programme of developing scientific knowledge, and the power it confers, for the supply of human needs and the relief of human ills. Much that we all value in modern civilization has resulted from it. But it was fatally flawed. It saw no value in nature other than its usefulness for practical human ends.

The interpretation of dominion as stewardship arose in this context in seventeenth-century England. Those who espoused it, most notably the eminent lawyer Matthew Hale, shared the contemporary enthusiasm for the extension of human control over nature, but instead of thinking purely of a human right to use nature for human benefit, they maintained also a human responsibility to care for nature. In the England of the early Royal Society (formed 1660), stewardship was an alternative to the excessively anthropocentric Baconian view. It recognized ethical obligations arising from nature's intrinsic value as created by God for God's glory, not merely for human benefit. As stewards responsible to the divine King, humans must administer the Earth justly and without cruelty. But it is important to recognize that the image of stewardship was intended positively to stress the human obligation to manage the natural world for its own good. It takes for granted that human control improves nature. Nature left to itself would be chaotic, a prey to its wilder elements. It needs a superior creature to keep it in order. Hence, no less than Baconianism, the idea of stewardship treated human supremacy over nature as an unquestioned good and technological advance as of unqualified value. As yet there was no recognition that human control of nature could be destructive, that wilderness might be better left alone than improved by human management, or that nature might have its own order that human technological interference can turn to chaos.

Stewardship came into its own again in Christian responses to the ecological crisis, and, not least, responses to the charge that it was the

Christian idea of human dominion over nature which was ultimately responsible for the ecological crisis. Its attraction is that it calls for human power over nature to be exercised responsibly, not exploitatively, and recognizes an intrinsic value in the non-human creation other than its usefulness to humans. It is only one of the ways in which the Genesis notion of dominion has been interpreted so as to avoid the implication of domination for purely human ends. Others have proposed that we see humans as co-creators with God (e.g. Arthur Peacocke), priests of creation (e.g. Colin Gunton), guardians of creation (Lawrence Osborn) or servants of creation (Andrew Linzey), but stewardship remains the most popular image, at least in evangelical contributions to the discussion. If we examine the way the *Declaration* understands it, we can see a notable shift from the emphasis in its seventeenth-century pioneers. The role of human stewards is not portrayed as improving nature, but as preserving and protecting it. The emphasis is on the givenness of the created order rather than on human intervention to change nature. It is not that nature needs human protection from its own destructiveness, but that it needs protection and healing from human abuse of it. Stewardship has acquired a late-twentieth-century content, along with somewhat chastened and humbled aims by comparison with the technological confidence it expressed in the days of the scientific revolution.

So, when the *Declaration* imagines the world as a garden to be tended by its human stewards (as in the final statement of the *Declaration*), we should probably not be thinking of a Renaissance garden, with its organization of nature into blatantly human order, its geometrical shapes and its sculptured trees, its silent declaration that it is nature humanly improved that most delights the human eye. No doubt we should be thinking of the more natural appearance – however contrived – of much modern taste in gardens. Perhaps we should even think of the ecologically correct garden in which at least a patch of protected wildness offers a semi-natural habitat for threatened wildlife. But hesitation about this arises from the *Declaration*'s statement that 'The earthly result of human sin has been a perverted stewardship, a patchwork of garden and wasteland in which the waste is increasing.' Here it seems that nature is either garden (humanly tended) or wasteland (humanly devastated). Wilderness (left alone by humans) is not envisaged. Of course, it is true that wilderness can now survive only if humans protect it from human interference. But, unlike the garden, its value is wholly independent of any human part in it. In the urgent need to protect the last great wildernesses – Antarctica and the depths of the oceans, not to mention the moon – the image of the garden may not be the most helpful, despite its Edenic precedent. This is not to deny that much of the natural world that we cherish and seek now to preserve is far from sheer wilderness, but rather the result of millennia of human occupation and modification. Gardens of all kinds are good, but they are not the only sort of good place. The challenge of the last wildernesses is one we have scarcely faced before in human history. Until recently wildernesses were just always there outside our garden fences or ha-has (changing attitudes to wilderness to be seen just in those changing forms of boundary). The question today is whether, now that we have the power to interfere everywhere on Earth (and even beyond), we can learn to care without interfering, simply to keep away and to keep our hands off – not so that we still have wildernesses to visit as eco-friendly tourists, but actually because God's other creatures have their own value for God and for themselves, quite independently of us.

I wonder whether the image of stewardship, like that of the garden, is entirely adequate to the use to which the *Declaration* tries to put it. I wonder if it does not come to us still too freighted with the baggage of the modern project of technological domination of nature. Can we entirely free it of the implication that nature is always better off when managed by us, that nature needs our benevolent intrusions, that it is our job to turn the whole world into a well-tended garden inhabited by well-cared-for pets? The problem is in part that stewardship remains – as so many inter-pretations of the Genesis 'dominion' have been – an image that depicts our relationship to the rest of creation in an entirely 'vertical' way. It sets us above the rest of creation, sharply differentiated from it, in God-given charge of it. (Notice that the *Declaration*, although it properly stresses that humans too are creatures, constantly refers to what I call 'the rest of creation' or 'the non-human creation' as simply 'creation', and just once as 'the rest of creation'. This is a verbal convenience, but not without a subliminal message.)

The 'vertical' relationship is undoubtedly one aspect of the biblical portrayal of the relationship of humans to the rest of creation. But there are also other aspects which place us alongside other creatures as fellow-creatures. Once we move on from Genesis 1:26–28 to the rest of the Bible, these other aspects seem to become actually more important than the idea of dominion, however we understand it. In what sense does Job have dominion over the other creatures to whom God so graphically and incisively draws his attention in chapters 37 – 39? The whole point is that he does not, that he has no bearing on the value and purpose of their existence for God's and their own sake. The lesson is to teach him his place as one creature among others in a creation of which he is not the be-all and end-all. Psalm 104 treats humans (v. 23) simply as one of the many kinds of living creatures for whom God provides. It depicts the world as a shared home for the many kinds of living creatures, each with its God-given place. Here, if anywhere in Scripture, is the basis for the image with which the *Declaration* ends, depicting the world not only as the garden we tend, but also as 'our earthly home'. But the ecological potential of this image is missed. Biblically, the Earth is not exclusively our home, but the home we share with God's many other creatures. Not only devastation, but even too much gardening can spoil it as a home for these others, even it seems to improve it for us.

Most important among the Bible's ways of placing us among the creatures, not over them, is the theme of creation's worship of God, portrayed in the Psalms (e.g. Ps. 148) and, with Christological and eschatological character, in the New Testament (Phil. 2:10; Rev. 5:13). All creatures, animate and inanimate, worship God. This is not, as modern biblical interpreters so readily suppose, merely a poetic fancy or some kind of primitive animism. The creation worships God just by being itself, as God made it, existing for God's glory. Only humans desist from worshipping God; other creatures, without having to think about it, do so all the time. There is no indication in the Bible of the notion that the other creatures need us to voice their praise for them. This idea, that we are called to act as priests to nature, mediating, as it were, between nature and God, is quite often found in recent Christian writing, but it intrudes our inveterate sense of superiority exactly where the Bible will not allow it. If creation needs priests, they are the four living creatures around God's throne (Rev. 4:6–8), only one of which has a human face, acting as our representative worshipper in heaven, whereas the others represent the animal creation with no need of human help. If anything, we should think of the rest of creation assisting our worship (in Ps. 148, the human praise follows the worship by all other creatures, from the angels downwards). But the key point is that implicit in these depictions of the worship of creation is the intrinsic value of all creatures, in the theocentric sense of the value given them by their Creator and offered back to him in praise. In this context, our place is beside our fellow-creatures as fellow-worshippers. In the praise in which we gratefully confess ourselves creatures of God, there is no place for hierarchy. Creatureliness levels us all before the otherness of the Creator.

In the pre-modern period creation's praise of God had a much more important place in the consciousness and the liturgy of the church than it has retained in the modern period. It functioned as a powerful corrective to the current notion that creation exists for human use. It is no accident that it features prominently in the life and work of Francis of Assisi, who also, famously, treated all fellow-creatures (inanimate as well as animate) as his brothers and sisters in the community of creation, and interpreted the human dominion over other creatures accordingly. Less well remembered (though many have heard of his cat Jeoffry) is the deeply Christian poetry of the eighteenth-century poet Christopher Smart, expressing a highly distinctive sense of the praise of God by all the extraordinary variety of God's creatures.[1] It is surely in the rediscovery of creation's worship that Christians today will come to appreciate most appropriately the value of all the creatures.

This 'horizontal' relationship with our fellow-creatures is essential to proper interpretation of what Genesis calls our dominion over them. Awareness of the horizontal relationship makes the vertical relationship, whatever we call it, rather like kingship as the book of Deuteronomy interprets it in a move designed to subvert all ordinary notions of rule (17:14–20). If Israel must have a king, then the king must be a brother. He is a brother set over his brothers and sisters, but still a brother, and forbidden any of the ways in which rulers exalt themselves over and entrench their power over their subjects. His rule becomes tyranny the moment he forgets that the horizontal relationship of brother/sisterhood is primary, kingship secondary.

We must recognize that most interpretations of the Genesis 'dominion' have proved dangerously open to abuse, pandering to human hubris and anthropocentrism, sanctioning much that we now, in a *Declaration* such as this, wish to repudiate. The concept of stewardship itself certainly cannot do all the work of radically reorientating our attitudes to the rest of creation that urgently needs to be done. Not everyone understands it as the *Declaration* does, with its emphasis on protection and preservation rather than intrusive management and restless improvement. We need more explicitly and unambiguously to distinguish the care of creation which the

Declaration commends, not only from the now obvious sins of waste, pollution and destruction, but also from the fundamental ideology that has driven the whole modern project of technological domination and, though weakened, still stalks the corridors of power and furnishes the unquestioned assumptions of many a scientist, Christians undoubtedly among them. It is the old Renaissance dream of humans as the gods of this world, its all-wise and all-powerful rulers, exercising divine creativity in remaking the world to their own design, treating nature as the raw material from which to create a world more adapted to its purely human ends. Biotechnology is the proof that this dream is now entering a whole new phase of attempted realization. Unmentioned in the *Declaration*, biotechnology is the battlefield on which we are already losing the struggle for the care of creation at the beginning of the third millennium.

10
God's covenant and our responsibility

Jürgen Moltmann

Jürgen Moltmann is one of the leading theologians of the present age. Until his retirement he was Professor of Systematic Theology at the University of Tübingen. His Gifford Lectures, God in Creation (1985), have been widely influential in stimulating theological study of environmental questions.

I would like to begin by identifying what impresses me in this *Declaration* and its importance for the continuing ecumenical discussions on ecology; and, secondly, I want to offer three proposals of my own in order to clarify a few points.

The *Declaration* gives a fresh perspective on the ecological problems of the modern world, by presenting them through the experience of the healing God. In Christ Jesus we experience not only the forgiveness of our sins but also the healing of our wounds. It is only logical to 'extend Christ's healing to the suffering creation'. 'By his wounds we are healed,' said the prophet in Isaiah 53:5, and in Colossians 1:20 we read that God was pleased 'through him [Christ] to reconcile to himself all things, whether things on earth, or things in heaven, by making peace through his blood, shed on the cross'.

The first declaration on ecology by the Protestant churches in Germany in 1979 spoke about 'reconciliation with nature': 'modern human beings and their modern world are not only alienated from God and from each other but also from nature. Reconciliation with God must therefore also lead to a reconciliation with nature.' This is good, but not enough, because the Bible suggests that nature itself is deeply hurt and wounded by human sins, and is 'groaning in travail'. It is very helpful to complement the perspective of 'reconciliation' with the perspective of 'healing'. The World Alliance of Reformed Churches made a proposal in 1990 on the 'Rights of Future Generations and the Rights of Nature', specifically to extend the 1948 United Nations Universal Declaration of Human Rights and to add to the 1980 UN World Charter for Nature with its new formulation in Rio in 1992. This legal aspect is important, and I shall return to the 'rights of nature' later. Last but not least, the Latin American liberation theologians have, after some hesitation, also picked up the ecological problems and dealt with them under the perspective of the 'liberation of nature'. This is another important aspect of the great chapter 8 in Romans: 'The creation itself will be liberated from its bondage to decay and brought into the glorious freedom of the children of God' (8:21).

We need more than one perspective to understand the richness of God's salvation, and 'Christ's healing of the suffering creation' is a significant addition.

The *Declaration* analyses correctly the interdependence of poverty and environmental degradation. Indira Gandhi once said, 'Poverty is the worst pollution.' And she was right. We can see environmental catastrophes everywhere in the Third World – and we can also see how much the industries of the 'First World' have been guilty of environmental devastation there. The toxic disaster in Bhopal was one example of this. Deforestation and monocultures in Third World countries have made much land uninhabitable. The *Declaration* is very outspoken on this point. It recalls the 'Oxford Declaration on Christian Faith and Economics' of January 1990, which challenged all of us, especially those in economic and political power in the First World, about our 'responsibility'.[1] Responsibility has two sides: we are responsible both to someone and for something. If we realize that it is God, Creator of heaven and Earth, who is making us responsible to himself, the extent of the things for which we are responsible to him and the extent of the things for which we ourselves are responsible also become clear: we are responsible for that part of God's creation over which we human beings can rule. Before God we are responsible for the Earth and its creatures to 'protect and heal' as much as we can. We need an ethic of responsibility for future generations and the future of the Earth; we must therefore overcome the hedonism of the consumer society, lest we become blind and numb and careless. One consequence of the ethics and politics of responsibility is a commitment to sustainable development, for a new, humble lifestyle, and for more respect for the presence of God in all things he has created.

The *Declaration* acknowledges the cosmic Christology of Colossians and thus supports most of the ecumenical churches, especially the Orthodox Church, where the cosmic and universal dimensions of Christ are always present in liturgy and theology. On Easter Sunday we praise God as we celebrate with the Risen One the healing of the whole groaning creation; with a cosmic Christology we await also a new creation (Rev. 21:5).

Environmental problems are not limited to the environment, but are signs of the sickness of our whole culture and the human 'sickness unto death'. The *Declaration* rightly calls for a rebirth of our relationship to God, to each other and to the community of all God's creatures.

I would like to focus on three needs: a new cosmic spirituality; human beings and nature in covenant with God; and the Sabbath of the Earth.

1. A new cosmic spirituality

The *Declaration* says: 'God is transcendent ... and immanent ...' Christian theological understanding is that creation is a Trinitarian process: God the Father creates through the Son – the Logos or Wisdom – by the energies of the Holy Spirit. Seen from the human point of view, this means that all things are created *by* God, formed *through* God and exist *in* God. The triune God stands over against the creation as Creator, resides in the creation as divine Logos or Wisdom, and fills the whole Earth with the dynamic energies of the Holy Spirit. Christ is the divine mystery of the world. Christ is present in every created being. In the apocryphal *Gospel of Thomas*, logion 77, Jesus says:

> I am the light that is over all,
> I am the universe: the universe has gone out from me,
> and the universe has returned to me again.
> Cleave the wood and I am there.
> Lift up a stone and there you shall find me.

In other words, whoever reverences Christ also reverences all creatures in him; Christ is in everything created. What we do to the Earth we do to Christ.

Where God's Word and Wisdom is, there God's Spirit is also. According to Genesis 1:2, creation through the Word is preceded by the presence of the energizing power of God's Spirit. God creates everything through his naming, differentiating and judging words. But God speaks always through the breath of his Spirit. The Word specifies and differentiates, the Spirit joins and forms the harmony. 'God breathes through all creation', says an English hymn. Through Word and Spirit, God the Creator is immanently present in his creation.

The book of Wisdom says: 'Lord, thou art the lover of life, thy immortal Spirit is in all things' (12:1). It seems to be a special work of the Spirit to sustain each creature and to keep the creation-community together.

In cosmic spirituality we recognize and revere God's presence in every creature and hence implement the creation-community. Human culture and the nature of this planet Earth can thus find a new sustainable harmony. This discovery will lead to a new role for the church. She will not only be a community of believers; her scope, in other words, will not be limited to the human world alone. The church will live out its recognition that salvation is not merely a matter of the soul, restricted to human beings. The church of Christ will know herself in the light of God's Word and Spirit as the advance radiance and beginning of God's presence in Glory, through the new creation of all things. The church of the cosmic Christ will be oriented towards the whole of the cosmos, and therefore be in fellowship with the groaning creatures and the wounded and crying Earth today. The ecological crisis of earthly creation is the church's own crisis too. When weak creatures die, the whole creation-community suffers. The church, seeing itself as representing the cosmos, will have to share this pain of the creatures in public protest. It is not just 'our human environment' that is suffering, because the creation is 'God's environment'. Every intervention in nature which can never be made good again is not merely a crime against humanity, but a sacrilege too. John Wesley said two centuries ago that the contemporary reckless and nihilistic destruction of nature is atheism in practice. Time has not changed the situation.

2. Human beings and nature in covenant with God

The *Declaration* speaks about God's 'covenant with all creatures'. I would like to expand this by quoting again from the 1990 Declaration of the World Alliance of Reformed Churches: 'We believe that God loves his creatures and wants to bring their lives to their full development and flowering. In God's eyes nothing created is a matter of indifference. Every creature has its own dignity and its own rights, which must be respected by the human creatures. That is what is said in the story about Noah: Behold, says God, I establish my covenant with you and your descendants after you and with every living creature (Gen. 9:9–10).'

It is this divine covenant *with us* which provides the basis for *human rights* in our human dignity. Out of the covenant with us and *our descendants after us* follow the *rights of future generations*; out of this covenant with us and our descendants after us and *every living creature* follow the *rights of nature*. Before God the Creator we and our descendants and all living things are partners in the same covenant. Nature is not our property, neither are we only part of nature. All living beings are partners in God's covenant, each in its own way. All living beings must therefore be respected by us as partners in God's covenant. 'Mankind is part of nature,' says the preamble of the UN World Charter for Nature. 'Every form of life is unique, warranting respect regardless of its worth to man.' This moral appeal, right though it is in itself, needs to be given a legal basis, so that nature is not dependent on the goodwill of human beings, but is recognized as an independent subject, with its own rights. On these grounds, I propose that the following sentences should be included in national constitutions:

> The natural world is under the special protection of the government. Through the way in which it acts, the state shows respect for the natural environment and protects it from exploitation and destruction by human beings *for its own sake*.

The German Animal Protection Act of 1986 is a good example of such an approach, because it views animals not merely as human property, but as 'fellow-creatures' of human beings: 'The purpose of this law is to protect the life and well-being of the animal through human responsibility for it is a fellow-creature. No-one may inflict pain, suffering or harm on an animal without reasonable grounds.'

To call animals 'fellow-creatures' is to recognize the Creator, the creature and the creation-community. The theological word 'creation' is more appropriate than the philosophical word 'nature' because it shows respect for God's rights to his creation, and therefore restricts the rights of human beings. God alone has the right of ownership; human beings can have only the right of use.

3. The Sabbath of the Earth

The Sabbath legislation of the Old Testament is full of ecological wisdom, leading to a special blessing for humankind and the Earth. As long as we see nature and our own bodies only through the dominating influence of work, we perceive only the utilitarian aspect of nature and only the instrumental side of our bodies. We find wisdom to understand nature and ourselves as God's creation when we celebrate the Sabbath/Sunday as a day of rest on which human beings and animals find peace and leave nature outside in peace. God the Creator 'finished' the creation of the world by celebrating the world's Sabbath. Through resting on the seventh day God blessed the whole creation by his silent presence.

The command to keep the Sabbath day holy (Exod. 20:8–11) is the longest of the Ten Commandments and arguably thus the most important. The blessing of the day includes men and women, parents and children, master and servants, residents and aliens – and the animals in the household. It is truly universal.

The significance of the Sabbath year for the land is ecologically even more important: 'In the seventh year the land is to have a sabbath of rest, a sabbath to the LORD' (Lev. 25:4). The reason given in Exodus 23:11 is a social one: 'then the poor among your people may eat'; in Leviticus 25:1ff. it is ecological: 'that the land itself must observe a sabbath to the LORD'. Such Sabbath rest for the land is important: all God's blessings are experienced by the obedient, but the disobedient will be punished.

In Leviticus 26:33ff. we read, 'And I will scatter you among the nations ... and your land will be laid waste, and your cities will lie in ruins.' Why? 'Then the land will enjoy its sabbath years all the time that it lies desolate and you are in the country of your enemies; then the land will rest and enjoy its sabbath.' This is indeed a remarkable ecological interpretation of Israel's Babylonian exile. God wanted to save his land, so he permits his people to be deported for 'seventy years', that is to say, until the land has had time to recover its health. We should be warned by this old story: uninterrupted exploitation of the land will lead to exile of its inhabitants, and ultimately to the disappearance of human beings from the Earth. At that time, God's Earth will celebrate the great Sabbath to the Lord, which modern humanity had denied it.

If we want our children to survive, we should be warned and permit the land 'to have a sabbath of rest' and restore its health again and again.

How would it be if we were to add to the great festivals of the church year (Christmas, Easter and Pentecost) an 'Earth Day' to celebrate creation? An 'Earth Day' of this kind is already celebrated by many Christian congregations in America on 22 April. How would it be if in Europe we were to declare 27 April, the day of the Chernobyl disaster, such a day?

On 'Earth Day' we should bow and beg forgiveness for the injustice we have inflicted on the Earth, so that we humans may once more be accepted into the community of the Earth; on 'Earth Day' we could be challenged anew to renew the covenant which God made with Noah and the Earth.

11

The Earth under threat

Ghillean T. Prance

Ghillean T. Prance retired in 1999 after twelve years as Director of the Royal Botanic Gardens, Kew. Prior to that, he was Senior Vice-President for Science at the New York Botanic Garden, and Director of the Institute of Economic Botany. He is the leading international authority on the composition and taxonomy of the Amazonian rainforest. Sir Ghillean has written widely on the ethics of conservation and the consequences of environmental mismanagement. He is the author of The Earth under Threat: A Christian Perspective *(1996).*

Introduction

As a Christian who is deeply involved in environmental matters, both in my daily work and because of my conviction that creation care is a Christian responsibility, I really welcome the *Declaration* and was enthusiastic to endorse it when it was first issued. In the *Declaration* we, as evangelical Christians, are showing the world that biblical faith can be a positive force for the solution of the environmental crisis rather than the negative force that it has often been accused of by such critics as Lynn White.

I should like to make my comments mainly on the third highlighted point in the *Declaration*, which reads:

> Many concerned people, convinced that environmental problems are more spiritual than technological, are exploring the world's ideologies and religions in search of non-Christian spiritual resources for the healing of the earth. As followers of Jesus Christ,

we believe that the Bible calls us to respond in four ways ...

The four ways are set out elsewhere in the volume (see p. 19); I shall return to them at the end of this comment.

The seriousness of the environmental crisis

It is not necessary to repeat details of the environmental crisis facing the world today, but I must state that it truly is grave. As a tropical-rainforest specialist, I see about 1% of the remaining forest disappearing each year. That is some 22 hectares a minute. Tropical rainforest covers only 7% of the land surface of the planet, yet harbours about 60% of the species. Can it be good stewardship to send all this into extinction? I have written about pollution, global warming and other environmental problems (Prance 1996); my purpose here is not to give a detailed catalogue of environmental damage, but merely to state that the crisis is so serious that scientific and political solutions alone are unlikely to address it satisfactorily. The magnitude of the problem demands ethical, moral and religious solutions as well as science. It is therefore encouraging to find an increasing number of secular writers and documents acknowledging that only a realization of the moral issues involved will produce satisfactory long-term solutions to the problem. This is a challenge to which Christianity must respond, and putting the *Declaration* to work is one way in which we can do so.

The secular response to the environmental crisis

A few quotations from recent secular writings show that the world is appealing to religion to help solve the environmental problem.

> In the final analysis, our economic and social behaviour is rooted in our deepest moral and spiritual motivations. We cannot expect to make the fundamental changes needed in our economic life unless they are based on the highest and best of our moral, spiritual and ethical traditions, a reverence for life, a respect for each other, and a commitment to responsible stewardship of the Earth. The transition to a sustainable society must be undergirded by a moral, ethical and spiritual revolution which places these values at the centre of our individual and societal lives (Strong 1993).[1]

It is not the ecologists, engineers, economists or earth scientists who will save spaceship earth, but the poets, priests, artists and philosophers (Hamilton 1993: 1).

However, in the last analysis, it is true that the scientific, technological, or economic solutions even in concert cannot do the job, because they will not be applied in a timely manner or sufficient in thoroughness unless humankind commits itself to a moral imperative to conserve life. 'No survival without a world ethic', says Hans Küng, Director of the Institute for Ecumenical Research at the University of Tübingen, Germany (Küng 1991). (See Hamilton 1993: 10.)

The ethic is founded on a belief in people as a creative force, and in the value of every human individual and each human society. It recognizes the interdependence of human communities, and the duty each person has to care for other people and for future generations. It asserts our responsibility towards the other forms of life with which we share this planet. It also recognizes that nature has to be cared for in its own right and not just as a means of satisfying human needs ...

We need to re-state and win support for the ethic of living sustainably because it is morally right.

Establishment of the ethic needs the support of the world's religions because they have spoken for centuries about the individual's duty of care for fellow humans and of reverence for divine creation. It also needs the backing of secular groups concerned with the principles that should govern relationships among people, and with nature. Such alliances will be timely and right even if the first purpose of religious and humanist groups are [sic] not the same as those of this strategy.

Action is therefore needed to: establish purposeful communication among religious leaders and thinkers, moral philosophers, leaders of organizations concerned with conservation and development, and politicians and writers concerned with the principles of human conduct; continue the process by which major religions have begun to identify and emphasize the elements of their faith and teachings that establish a duty and care for nature;

involve people in the development of the world ethic through existing religions and citizens' groups and through environmental and humanitarian non-governmental organizations (*Caring for the Earth* 1991).

Even a population summit of fifty-eight of the world's national scientific academies did not claim that science alone would resolve the population crisis:

> Furthermore it is not prudent to rely on science and technology alone to solve problems created by rapid population growth, wasteful resource consumption and poverty.
>
> Scientists, engineers, and health professionals should study and provide advice on: cultural, social, economic, religious, educational and political factors that affect reproductive behaviour, family size and successful family planning (US National Academy, 1993).

> If environmental degradation were purely, or even primarily, a problem demanding scientific or technological solutions, then its resolution would probably have been accomplished by now. As it is, however, our crises of pollution and resource depletion reflect profound difficulties with some of the most basic principles in our accepted system of values. They challenge us to assess the adequacy of these principles and, if need be, to discover a new framework for describing what it means to behave ethically or to be a 'moral' person (Shrader-Frechette 1981).

There is obviously a growing realization in the secular world that the environmental crisis is indeed a moral issue, and so the world is turning to religious leaders and philosophers for help. This is a challenge to which Christians must be in the forefront of the response if there is to be any lasting and serious commitment to responsible, sustainable stewardship of our planet. If we do not respond, our place will be taken by false gods and other religions that worship creation rather than the Creator.

The Christian response

In response to the many people who are exploring the world's ideologies and religions in search of resources for healing the Earth, the Christian *Declaration* calls for repentance, for action, for examination of the biblical basis for creation care, and for investigation of what creation reveals to us about God. If we were to do all these things, then Christians would be in the forefront of the environmental movement rather than leaving the action to the pagans.

We have indeed forgotten that 'the earth is the Lord's' and that this means we should care for it. Repentance for our neglect is the obvious first step for any meaningful action. Once we realize the gravity of our neglect of creation, the only way towards Christian Earth-keeping is through biblical study, so that our actions are rooted in the fullness of God's revelation in Christ and through the Scriptures.

'For he [Christ] is the image of the invisible God, the firstborn of all creation; for in him all things in heaven and on earth were created ...' (Col. 1:15–16, NRSV). Creation is waiting 'with eager longing for the revealing of the children of God' (Rom. 8:19, NRSV), yet we, the children of God, have been all too slow to respond. The fact that the world is calling us to respond makes the situation even more urgent. My hope is that *An Evangelical Declaration on the Care of Creation* will lead to this response because we know and worship the Creator, and that we will not leave it to those who often worship creation and have no respect for the Creator. Surely we can do a better and more respectable job.

12

A universal as well as an evangelical *Declaration*

Howard J. Van Till

Howard J. Van Till was Professor of Physics at Calvin College in Michigan from 1967 until 1999. He has been a long-term activist in demolishing the barriers between science and the Christian faith, in particular with his authorship or collaboration in The Fourth Day: What the Bible and the Heavens are Telling Us about the Creation *(1986),* Science Held Hostage: What's Wrong with Creation Science and Evolutionism? *(1988), and* Portrait of Creation: Biblical and Scientific Perspectives on the World's Formation *(1990).*

On pragmatic considerations alone, the human race as a whole has ample reason to attend to the care of the world that we inhabit. A well-tended environment provides a wholesome setting for life, both now and in the future. We want to breath clean air, to drink clean water, and to live as healthy members of a robust ecosystem. It makes sense, therefore, that the global human community would want to articulate a set of constructive criteria for our use of natural resources and our management of the biosphere. Even the vast differences among human cultures and religions, interesting and important as they are, should not stand as barriers on the road towards global and long-term cooperation in maintaining a robust environment for future generations. Communal pragmatism would, I believe, provide a sufficient rationale for an international effort to exercise care for the terrestrial biosphere.

Some persons might contest this brief statement, but I suspect that the vast majority of objections would come from persons who are willing to set aside global and long-term benefits for the sake of achieving local and short-term gains. Individual persons can, of course, choose to act selfishly and to exploit environmental resources, both animate and inanimate, for their short-term personal gain. Even individual nations can be motivated by a self-interest that has not been enlightened by a fitting sense of membership in a global community that values the thriving of future generations.

How might the global community deal with those people and nations who act selfishly? Should we preach the merits of an 'enlightened self-interest' that places the need to practise a communal pragmatism above the desire for individual gain? I suppose that could be done (and has already been tried), but my expectations for the success of such a preaching venture are quite dismal. Each one of us knows how tempting it is to 'look out for number one' with tireless vigour. Sacrificing personal comfort or gain for the sake of a global community might be a noble act, but it is not always an attractive choice. After all, a person might say, 'Just look at the way other individuals are acting. Why should I be motivated to give anything up for the sake of those despicable specimens of greed and environmental abuse?'

In a sense, *An Evangelical Declaration on the Care of Creation* constitutes an articulate and exemplary answer to this question of motivation. It is a carefully crafted call for the Christian community to act in the best interests of the global community, but for reasons vastly different from the enlightened self-interest of which we have so far been speaking. The *Declaration* calls for a certain style of life and action, not merely for pragmatic reasons, but as the manifestation of a robust set of religious beliefs that define the Christian community.

I note with appreciation that this *Declaration* speaks not merely of care of 'the environment', but of care of 'the creation'. As a member of the Christian community I consider it essential to employ the term 'creation' as the proper name of the world – the entire universe of which we and our terrestrial ecosystem are a part. Oddly enough, using this 'creation' label is sometimes misunderstood, at least in North America, and needs to be clarified.

What does it mean 'to create' something? I judge that the most fundamental meaning of 'to create' is 'to give being' in place of non-being. So defined, the term speaks of the uniquely divine action of a Creator, an action without an exact counterpart in the spectrum of human actions.

Those things that we often call human 'creations' are, I believe, better seen as 'actualizations of potentialities' that were already resident within the created world. Thus, for us to produce an artefact of human craftsmanship or artistry – a product of the action of our hands or minds – is to actualize some object or work of art that was already potentially present in the created world. In contrast, 'the creation', as the term is employed in the *Declaration*, is the totality of what has been given being by the Creator – the entire robust system of substances, capabilities and potentialities that characterize the world of which we are a part.

I find it essential to distinguish the uniquely divine act of *creation* – the giving of being – from the various creaturely processes and events that comprise the *formational history* of the universe or of the living organisms that inhabit our portion of it. The creation/evolution controversy that continues to rage in North America is mostly a shouting match about the character of the world's formational history. Some (but certainly not all) Christians choose to picture the creation's formational history in a way that focuses especial attention on the concept of occasional episodes of divine form-imposing action. This is commonly known as the 'special creationist' perspective. Why would there be a need for these special, form-imposing acts? Was the creation not sufficiently equipped from the outset with the formational capabilities for actualizing certain forms? In the minds of some, evidently not. A number of Christians have argued that there is empirical evidence in support of this claim for the absence of key formational capabilities. Consequently, they assert that the evolutionary development of life-forms as envisioned by biological science is thereby made impossible.

Other Christians (myself included) have chosen to envision the creation's formational history in a way that celebrates all of the creation's remarkable capabilities for organizing and transforming itself into the whole array of physical structures (such as galaxies, stars and planets) and the multifarious forms of life that exist and have existed. We have no substantive reason to promote any particular one of the scientific theories that contribute to the evolutionary paradigm, but we find the general theoretical picture to be the best way of accounting for the empirical data at hand. In order for the evolutionary development of physical structures and life-forms to be possible, the creation must be richly gifted with a robust economy of formational capabilities. But if those capabilities are 'gifts of being' given to the creation by its Creator, why should that not be the case? Should not each of the creation's formational capabilities be celebrated as a manifestation of the Creator's incomprehensible creativity in conceptualizing a system that could function so fruitfully? And should not the entire menu of the creation's formational capabilities be taken as evidence of the Creator's generosity in giving the universe such fullness of being? The creation of which the *Declaration* speaks has, I believe, been generously gifted by its Creator with a wondrous array of capabilities for achieving its potentialities and fulfilling its Creator's intentions.

Why should evangelical Christians care for the world in which we live? Stated as simply as possible, because it is 'the creation', the luxuriant garden given to us by our generous Creator. One of the basic tenets of Christian belief is that the world of which we are a part has being only because the God of whom the Hebrew and Christian Scriptures speak chose graciously to give it being 'in the beginning' and to continue to sustain it in being from moment to moment. Caring for it is, therefore, no mere matter of global pragmatism. Caring for the creation is for the Christian but one element in an integrated package of appropriate responses to the knowledge of who we are. From the Christian perspective, caring for the creation is an essential act of worship – our public declaration that God is deserving of our unrestrained praise, thanksgiving and service. The exploitation or abuse of the creation by other persons does not exempt the Christian from the call to care for it with diligent and sustained effort. Neither can the call be set aside as something only for other members of the community to pay heed to. Each member of the larger Christian community is called to express worship of the Creator, which includes the care of the creation.

The *Declaration* is, I believe, to be commended for avoiding one of the pitfalls of attitude found in some portions of the evangelical Christian community. There is a song, familiar to North American evangelicals, that includes the sentiment, 'This world is not my home, I'm just a-passing through ... And I can't feel at home in this world anymore.' Looking forward to the life to come may be admirable, but does that warrant a deprecatory attitude towards our life on Earth? I presume that it does not. Whatever the *Declaration* can do to reverse any disposition to minimize the value of our earthly home would be most welcome. The creation, maintained in being by its Creator for thousands of millions of years, surely deserves a few years of our own creaturely effort as committed stewards, caretakers of God's garden. *An Evangelical Declaration on the Care of Creation* is a most eloquent expression of recognition that this position of stewardship is one to be treasured and to be practised as an act of grateful worship.

In addition to these words of commendation, let me voice a couple of concerns. First, is it possible that the *Declaration* is so focused on an evangelical Christian basis for caring for the creation that it minimizes the value of contributions that members of other faith communities might also make? I presume there was no intention to do so, but it could be so interpreted. Might it not be a good thing for members of diverse faith communities to take appreciative note of how their varied religious commitments lead in some instances to common goals for particular action? Might it not be a fruitful experience for members of these differing faith communities to work side by side for the responsible use of the world's resources and for the management of the global garden? When two persons work together for the benefit of others, something remarkably good can happen: walls of separation, of misunderstanding and of suspicion can be replaced by bridges of mutual respect and appreciation. In fairness to the *Declaration*, there is one entry that begins, 'We call upon Christians to listen to and work with all those who are concerned about the healing of creation ...' Thus the sentiment that I seek is there, but it seems a rather quiet whisper towards the closing of the document. I would respectfully suggest there is much that Christians could learn through partnership with members of other faith communities.

A second concern, quite different in character, has to do with the conjunction of boldness and risk that the making of this public *Declaration* represents. Where is the boldness? I see it in the intensity with which the claim is made for the *necessity* of the evangelical Christian perspective if the campaign for the care of the creation is to be successful. The *Declaration* states, for instance, that 'biblical faith is essential to the solution of our ecological problems'. Not merely important, but *essential.* That close connection of a biblically informed Christian faith and the proper care of the creation appears consistently throughout the *Declaration.* My point here is not to contest that these two form an inseparable union, but to note that it represents a strong and bold claim. Such boldness may serve well in communicating the urgency of this *Declaration* to members of the evangelical Christian community, but might it not also provide the occasion for offence to persons who are members of other faith communities? One hopes not.

Where is the risk? What could possibly be risky in the making of this

Declaration? Ironically, the risk may appear at the same point as the boldness. Perhaps that is an unavoidable circumstance when a faith community offers a public profession that spells out not only some of the tenets of its belief system, but also what is counted to be the behaviour pattern that necessarily follows from these beliefs.

I take fundamental beliefs to be a powerful factor in stimulating human behaviour. I take that to be so even when those beliefs lie unexamined below the level of conscious reflection. Some observers of human behaviour might argue that unexamined basic beliefs operate even more effectively than those principles that are publicly professed as beliefs. 'Beliefs' can be publicly expressed for numerous reasons other than their being the operative beliefs that govern actual behaviour. By this *Declaration*, the evangelical Christian community now places its behaviour on the line, open for public scrutiny and evaluation. Failure to behave in a manner consistent with this *Declaration* could rightly be taken as evidence for a disparity between actual beliefs and professed beliefs – saying the 'right' thing, but doing something entirely different.

My expectation is otherwise. The beliefs expressed in the *Declaration* are, I believe, both true to the Christian heritage and authentically held by the evangelical Christian community to which this call to action is directed. May the fruits of these beliefs now become an eloquent and effective witness to all who watch how we choose how to live our lives and to tend God's garden. May we be exemplary in the manner in which we gratefully employ the creation's gifts, and lovingly encourage its potentialities for serving the needs of 'all creatures great and small'.

13

Our common future

John T. Houghton

John T. Houghton is a former Professor of Atmospheric Physics at the University of Oxford who then became Director-General of the UK Meteorological Office (1983–91). He was Chairman of the Royal Commission on Environmental Pollution (1992–98) and has been Chairman of the Scientific Committee of the Inter-Governmental Panel on Climate Change (IPCC) since it was set up in 1988. Besides his scientific publications, Sir John is the author of Does God Play Dice? *(1988),* Global Warming *(1994), and* The Search for God: Can Science Help? *(1995).*

The challenge of global pollution

On a *local* scale, pollution of air, water or land due to human activities has been around for a long time. However, in many places during the past century, local air and water quality has been greatly improved. What has become increasingly apparent (even since the *Declaration* was issued in 1994), and what is adding urgency to environmental concern, is the presence of human activities that lead to pollution on the *global* scale. An example of this is the effect of small amounts of chemicals containing chlorine, such as the chlorofluorocarbons (CFCs), that cause damage of global extent to the ozone layer in the stratosphere (Brenton 1994). Another example relates to 'greenhouse gases' (GHGs), such as carbon dioxide, that spread through the whole atmosphere and result in climate change with its potential deleterious effects. The existence of global environmental problems requires solutions that are organized on a global scale. Scientists and policymakers worldwide have to respond to this imperative and find appropriate ways of meeting the challenge. The worldwide Christian community with its God-given mandate to care for creation also needs urgently to address this challenge and respond with appropriate action.

Not the only global problem

We hear a lot about 'globalization' and indeed we increasingly experience it, as information exchange, business, trade, and economics develop and are pursued on a worldwide scale. The environmental problems I have mentioned are not the only global problems; there are other issues of a global scale that also bear strongly on the global environment.

Two such issues are those of unsustainable population growth, largely in the developing world, and the unsustainable use of resources, largely in the developed world (see John Guillebaud's contribution, pp. 155–160). When these issues are put alongside each other, the disparity between the developed world and large parts of the developing world comes into sharp contrast. For instance, a child born in the United States consumes about one hundred times more resources than one born in Bangladesh.

A further issue is that of poverty. The gap between rich nations and poor nations is becoming wider. What is even more disturbing is the flow of wealth which, as a consequence of debt and the pattern of trade, is from countries that are poor to those that are comparatively rich – a situation that is condemned in Scripture in the strongest terms (Amos 6:4–7; Is. 10:1–3; Luke 6:20–25; and many other passages. See also Sider 1978).

Increasing poverty and the widening poor–rich divide seriously exacerbate environmental degradation, largely because people on the edge of subsistence can only give thought to their immediate needs and do not have the luxury of conserving their very limited resources or their environment. Many, including the Prince of Wales, have drawn attention to the strong links which exist between poverty, population growth and environmental degradation, and have argued that we will not succeed in protecting the environment until all these issues are addressed together (Prins 1993).

The term 'sustainable development' is constantly on the lips of politicians. It can be popularly defined as living so as not to cheat on our children or grandchildren. But both the sustainability and the development implied by the term must be put in the global context. *Intergenerational* equity is important and challenging. But much more challenging is *international* equity. The new millennium will be dominated by international issues. Both our relationships to our fellow-humans with whom we share our Earth, and our care for the rest of creation, have to be global in their scope.

A further global issue is that of global security. Our traditional understanding of security is based on the concept of the sovereign state with secure borders maintained by military means, but many global issues transcend national boundaries: communications, industry and commerce increasingly ignore state borders, as do environmental problems such as climate change. Recent wars have been concerned with protecting sources of oil; wars in the future may be fought over water, which is becoming increasingly scarce and often comes from sources which are shared between nations. When addressing the issue of global security, a broader strategy needs to be developed which considers *inter alia* environmental threats as a possible source of conflict. In addressing the appropriate action to combat such threats, it would be better overall, and more cost-effective in security terms, to allocate resources to the removal or alleviation of the threat, rather than to expensive military or other measures to deal head-on with the security problem itself (Julian Oswald, in Prins 1993: 113–134). The challenge to all countries is to begin to think and act in new ways.

The contribution of science and technology

In 'postmodern' society, objective scientific analysis and thinking do not have the dominant place they used to have. What is generally believed is much more subjective; it can even be what people wish to believe! The public or politicians often react to what the media say or to pressure groups (Gelbspan 1998); 'mad cow disease' and the proposed disposal in the North Sea of Shell's *Brent Spar* provide some recent examples. In our society, a particular challenge is to find ways in which science can speak with a clearer voice.

As scientific discovery has progressed, the order, reliability, consistency and unity of creation have been increasingly apparent. These objective qualities in the scientific description of things demonstrate the integrity of the universe. Christians associate these qualities with the reliability and consistency of God himself; our scientific and religious perceptions reinforce each other. Let me illustrate what I mean by this.

Many modern discoveries affirm the *unity* of creation. Cosmologists probing the extreme limits of the universe, over 10,000 million light years away in space and 10,000 million years away in time, find that the same physics apply to the period just after the Big Bang billions of years ago – and to the Earth today. Closer to home we are also becoming increasingly aware of the unity of the living creation – of the many interdependencies between different forms of life, and between living systems and the physical and chemical environment that surrounds life on the Earth. The Gaia theory expounded by James Lovelock (1979, 1988) and others has explored some of these scientific insights. We humans are closely dependent for our livelihood and survival on the rest of creation.

Science is the means by which humans gain understanding of creation, and it provides the basis for the assessment of environmental problems and for action. But associated with scientific knowledge there is un-certainty to a greater or lesser extent. The 'precautionary principle' has been formulated to take this uncertainty into account. A formulation of the principle found in the Framework Convention on Climate Change agreed at the Earth Summit in 1992 is: 'Where there are threats of serious or irreversible damage, lack of full scientific certainty shall not be used as a reason for postponing cost-effective measures to prevent environmental degradation.'

It is worth labouring this point, because experience shows that much of the difficulty that arises at the interface between science and politics comes from questions about risk and uncertainty. It is important that these questions are properly informed. The first essential is recognizing the objective nature of science, that science is not just a matter of opinion but has a basis in fact and testable evidence. But science is carried out by people, so there is a subjective context to it, a context that is particularly exposed when uncertainty is presented and discussed (Polanyi 1962). Personal judgment can be an important factor in the uncertainty debate; public perception needs also to be understood and openly taken on board (Royal Commission on Environmental Pollution 1998).

Three ingredients are essential to scientific assessment and to scientific or technological solutions to environmental problems. I have called them the three H's – honesty, holism and humility. Both environmental and anti-environmental lobby groups often exaggerate or distort in their efforts to get their message across. If science is to be credible, it has to be absolutely honest and properly balanced. The peer-review process in science is an effective way of weeding out much inadequate or distorted scientific work before it gets published. Thomas Henry Huxley emphasized a hundred years ago the need for scientists to be 'humble before the facts'. Important too is humility towards the Creator on whose behalf we are stewards, towards the rest of creation which we are mandated to serve, and towards other humans with whom we share the environment.

An example of how science can address a particular environmental problem and inform policymakers in an effective way is found in the Intergovernmental Panel on Climate Change (IPCC). I have been privileged to chair or co-chair the Panel's scientific assessments from its establishment in 1988. A large number of the world community of climate scientists, including the leading scientists in the field, have been involved in these assessments, as either authors or reviewers. Under the discipline of science with its honesty and integrity, a large measure of consensus has been achieved about what we know and where the major uncertainties lie. The relevance of the assessments to policymakers has been assured by involving them in the way the scientific information is presented. The assessments therefore have wide ownership, both in the world community of scientists and among policymakers. Because of this, they have been very influential in convincing governments and international agencies of the need for action.

Principles of Christian stewardship

Human care for creation is often described by the term 'stewardship'. When used in the secular world it is not clear on whose behalf we are acting as stewards. That is not a problem for the Christian (although see p. 102). 'The earth is the LORD's' (Ps. 24:1), and we have been instructed to look after the Earth on his behalf (Gen. 1:28; 2:15) But what is meant by the 'stewardship' of creation in a Christian context? At the very least, it means we must not damage the creation. As humans have become more numerous and machines have become more powerful, creation has been damaged in various ways and is now threatened by severe damage on a global scale – a situation that responsible stewardship must begin to reverse.

But Christian stewardship should be much more than the avoidance of damage. What about our responsibility for the non-human creation? It is sometimes argued that creation would be better off without humans. How, therefore, is the 'image of God', with which we were endowed at creation, to be apparent in the relationship of humans to creation?

One of the criticisms that is raised about the use of the word 'stewardship' to describe our relationship to creation (the term also being widely used in the secular world) is that it tends to put little emphasis on our responsibility for the non-human creation. In other words, it is too anthropocentric. Although most Christians accept that stewardship is probably the best word available, a large challenge to Christians is to think through more carefully the relationship with, and the responsibilities that God has given us for, the whole creation (see, for example, p. 136). That thinking then needs to be turned into clear practical application.

Partnership with God

The world is not short of statements of principles or of ideals. Thousands of pages of declarations, conventions and resolutions emanated from the Earth Summit in Rio in 1992 and have since been repeated and amplified by international or national bodies. What seems so often to be lacking is the resolve to carry them out. Sir Crispin Tickell, a British diplomat who was one of the architects of the Earth Summit, has commented, 'Mostly we know what to do but we lack the will to do it.'

Many recognize this lack of will as a 'spiritual' problem (using the word 'spiritual' in a general sense). We are only too aware of the strong temptations we experience at both the personal and national levels to use the world's resources to gratify our selfishness and greed. As we realize how formidable is the task of stewardship of the Earth, we may often feel that it is beyond the capability of the human race to tackle it adequately. But an important part of the Christian gospel is that we do not have to carry this responsibility on our own. Our partner is none other than God himself. The Genesis stories of creation contain a beautiful description of this partnership as they speak of God walking with Adam and Eve 'in the garden in the cool of the day' – no doubt discussing how they were getting on with the care of the garden. Moving to the New Testament, Jesus said to his disciples, 'Apart from me you can do nothing' (John 15:5). This is generally assumed to refer to non-material matters, but in the Christian message the material and the spiritual are closely linked. I believe that Jesus meant his remark to be a much more comprehensive statement, applying to all that we do. After all, taking care of the Earth is also very much God's work. A clear understanding of the responsibilities and abilities we have been given, coupled with trust in God's presence and faithfulness, is the mixture that makes stewardship of the Earth an exciting and challenging activity.

A Christian challenge to the world

In the Western world there are many material goals: economic growth, social welfare, better transport, more leisure and so on. But, for our fulfilment as human beings, we desperately need not just material challenges, but challenges of a moral or spiritual kind. There are strong connections between our basic attitudes (including religious belief) and environmental concern. Many people in the world are already attempting to be good stewards of the Earth and are deeply involved in a host of ways in matters of environmental concern. Such concern could, however, with benefit to us all, be elevated to a higher public and political level. Al Gore (1992), US Vice-President, has proposed that all humans should embrace the preservation of the Earth as a new organizing principle. An appropriate challenge for everybody, from individuals, communities, industries and governments through to multinational companies, especially for those in the relatively affluent Western world, is to reject the parochial, selfish attitudes that are so dominant and to take on board this urgent task of the environmental stewardship of the whole of our Earth.

14

A new look at old passages

Peter Harris

Peter Harris is International Coordinator of the A Rocha Trust. He has four children, and together with his wife Miranda worked for twelve years in Portugal to establish and run the Trust's first field study centre and bird observatory. For the last three years they have been living in France working with national colleagues to establish a similar centre on the edge of the Camargue, while assisting emerging A Rocha projects elsewhere, notably in Lebanon, Kenya and the UK. Peter has experience of mission projects in Asia, Africa, the Middle East and South America, and is an adjunct faculty member of Regent College, Vancouver. He is an Anglican minister and author of Under Bright Wings *(1993.)*

I have to begin with a confession. When I saw *An Evangelical Declaration on the Care of Creation*, my heart sank. Here we go again, I thought, with yet more well-honed phrases in a virtual vacuum, and another delayed bandwagon for the lame to leap on. In general, evangelical Christians tend to be entirely indifferent to environmental issues, and, as truly evangelical declarations are best made principally by how we live (accompanied by explanations as appropriate), protestations on paper serve for very little. In my work with the A Rocha Trust, I have been working for the last fifteen years, first in Portugal and more recently in Lebanon, France, Kenya and the UK, to see how we could make a practical difference in caring for creation. We have studied a variety of threatened habitats, particularly wetlands, and have been working for their protection, principally through environmental research and education. Over most of those years, the distinctively Christian character of our work has been given a somewhat intrigued welcome by other environmental groups, although, with some startling exceptions (notably John Ball of Crosslinks, John Stott, and some of the contributors to this book), we have also encountered considerable evangelical incomprehension or worse.

So, in commenting on the *Declaration*, I have to face an uncomfortable paradox. There is an enormous amount to do in order to change the way we live as Christians. But I am more and more convinced that the urgent task in changing the way we live as evangelical Christians has to begin with believing differently, and not simply obeying new rules. It is not that we need to adopt an updated legalistic code for the contemporary Christian life: thou shalt recycle thy toothpaste tube, thou shalt not covet thy neighbour's bicycle, and thou shalt make sure everyone else notices that thy yoghurt is organic. As I have puzzled over the causes for current (not historic, incidentally) evangelical indifference to creation as we have encountered it with A Rocha, it has become uncomfortably clear that its roots lie in unbiblical belief. It is not that evangelicals shrink from paying a price in lost comfort for a change of lifestyle. There are many wonderful examples of how the Christian church worldwide lives very sacrificially in the face of human need, and in many places it is a compelling stimulus for social change and redemption. The problem is that we do not extend that commitment and concern to the wider creation, nor are we persuaded that God cares about it. And so a *Declaration* is maybe not such a bad beginning if we wish to change evangelical minds. It will be even better if those of us who support it are asked in a couple of years' time what actual difference it has made to our lives.

Does this *Declaration* do justice to the enormity of the theological and practical task, and does it give us a foundation for a better biblical understanding, and a guide to more biblical living? I believe it does, because where Christian indifference to creation seems to have begun is with the careless or wilful adoption of human-centred thinking into the heart of the church. The *Declaration* challenges that at every turn. It is somewhat of a cliché in Christian teaching that Enlightenment anthropocentrism became the measure of all things for Western society, including the church, and so human well-being was soon perceived as the aim of history. We have not, however, recognized so clearly that one result was a lusty sub-Christian version of related ideas that reduces the whole point of the gospel to human salvation. In its extreme manifestation, salvation becomes a kind of fashion accessory in the main project of our individual self-fulfilment: Gucci for the body, the media for the mind, and Jesus for the soul. Grateful for the crumbs falling from the postmodern table, the church has been tempted to settle happily into the role of provider of 'spiritual' need. In denial of the force of biblical argument, 'spiritual' becomes equated with 'non-material'.

Tragically, the truth is all the other way round. We find our identity as a result of discovering who God is – we are who we are because of him, rather than he being there for us. The foundational biblical affirmation about God is that he is the Creator, not only of the human race, but of all life and everything that is. Immediately this places us in a completely different relational context; no longer are we the starting-point of our existence, but we are the creation of God, together with not only everyone else on the planet, but all the universe. While this may seem abstract and high-flown, the Gospel of John with its abrupt juxtaposition of the cosmic with a crisis in the alcohol supply for a small-town wedding should alert us to the extremely mundane implications of major truths. To recognize God as being Creator of all rescues us in a very practical way from the working assumption of our times that the creation is there just for us.

But the biblical theology in the *Declaration* has other profound implications. Many of them derive from the affirmation of God's character as Creator and Redeemer of his creation.

God cares for all his creation, not only for its human component: 'God's concern is for all creatures,' as the *Declaration* says. However, it has to be said that the *Declaration*'s biblical justification for such an affirmation, from Genesis 1:31, is less convincing. The text records God's satisfaction with all he has made, but refers to creation before the fall. Over recent years, the fall has been the most convenient get-out for evangelical leaders looking for scanty rags of theology to cover naked free-market greed. By referring to this passage in Genesis, the *Declaration* allows a familiar side-step. The conventional argument is that now that creation is fallen, God has lost interest in everything but salvaging the souls of human beings; all we need to know is how to live in the creation in the meantime, and to extract what we can of God's good gifts from it before it all burns in the final judgment. In adducing texts carelessly, the *Declaration* plays into the hands of such shoddy exegesis, and slips into a bad evangelical habit. Ironically, our very loyalty to the authority of Scripture, as plainly stated at the beginning of the *Declaration*, has sometimes meant that arguments in the evangelical community degenerate into a sterile business of trading isolated texts; we are less familiar than other Christian traditions with the patient and thoughtful work of building a biblical theology that seeks to draw on the development of biblical thinking rather than lunging for isolated verses. At several points, and this is one of them, the *Declaration* needs some biblical theology rather than a text out of context, not least because the ideas being expounded are truly biblical. Psalm 104, written about the creation after the fall, might have given a more adequate testimony to God's love for all his creation as we know it. The Gospel writers depict Jesus' involvement with and lordship over the material world in many ways, but not least in the incarnation itself. We see the creation serving his loving purposes as Jesus stills the storm, and turns water to wine. His clothes and person are transfigured on the mountain, and throughout his ministry we see God's continuing love for all he has made. Even if human well-being were not intimately connected to the wider well-being of creation (and human suffering so often and so evidently is the result of its abuse), it would be incoherent to refuse to the wider creation the love the three-personed Creator pours out in its creation, never mind the meaning of its being subsequently held together 'in Christ', as Colossians explains.

However, a certain amount of shorthand is inevitable in a document such as the *Declaration*, and those who follow the trail of texts that appear throughout will find that they have been pitched into fruitful ground. More importantly, if the affirmations of the *Declaration* are taken seriously, they provide three particular possibilities for a wide-ranging renewal of evangelical belief that will inevitably change our discipleship in more biblical directions.

1. The fundamental question for anyone who cares about the creation is not 'What must we do about the environment?', but 'Who is God?' And the answer that the *Declaration* gives is powerfully framed, beginning by affirming that God is the Creator, first and foremost. Frequently evangelicals have been tempted to begin with human need, saying before anything that God is our saviour. The *Declaration* is more biblical and follows the classical scheme of creation, fall, redemption and final consummation in Christ. As the starting-point is therefore seen as the character of God, so the first response of the believer is not a fix-it activism, but true worship of God the Creator. In practical terms, this could change the culture of the evangelical world quite profoundly. Mark Noll

(1994) has lamented the selective pragmatism of evangelicalism. Seen positively, the roots of that pragmatism lie in a keen awareness of the acute needs of our fellow human beings, and the awareness of hope that the gospel brings. But negatively, it produces a lack of awareness of the priority of worship and prayer as the mainspring of any work, and of the character of work as true worship which is how Paul, the activist *par excellence*, describes it in Romans 12. If we learn to begin our reflection and our concern for change out of a vivid awareness of the character of God the Creator, and a longing to worship him, we will be less tempted to see our personal salvation as the beginning and end of the story, but rather as being the outworking of God's wider initiative of redemptive love for all he has made. Paradoxically, we will be very different if first of all we are worshippers, rather than activists, and if we understand that worship is not merely meetings or music, but is rather the life of God's people offered up to him in all its wholeness.

2. The *Declaration* takes a justified theological risk in saying 'we offer creation and civilization back in praise to the Creator'. If we as evangelicals begin to do that, it will signify a huge change. We are used to 'offering ourselves' as the church, but not to offering 'creation and civilization'. In that phrase lies the recognition of the lordship of Christ over all things, including culture and society. Evangelicals have lived very uneasily with that idea, not least in recent times, because of the very terrible nature of that culture and society. How, following the terrible events of two world wars, the multiple genocides of the twentieth century, and now widespread ecological catastrophe in so many areas, can we believe in God's kingdom except exclusively within the church? The answer is by the mark of engagement in a world that has not changed its character very much: that is, by the pattern of the cross. The calling of the church is redemptive suffering, in obedience to a holy God who stands against human rebellion and for those seeking him in faith. This is part at least of what Paul writes about in Romans 8, where he describes us groaning as creation groans, waiting for adoption and redemption.

So the *Declaration* invites us into a renewal of our relationship with creation. If God cares for all he has made, so must we. If the wider creation is included in his eternal purposes of redemption, then our dealings with the material world in all its forms assume a quite different significance. But in practice we recognize our relationship to God most acutely in our relationships to people and to the church, the body of Christ; this has allowed us to consign whole areas of human activity and experience to an area which has little to do with God or our relationship with him. Hence the exodus of Christian thinking (although not necessarily of Christian people) from the arts, environmental issues, business practices, and legal and educational priorities. So actually this little *Declaration* begins to look like a very subversive document indeed. If what is at issue is the potential recovery of the lordship of Christ in every area of life, then our relationship to the societies we live in, and their physical environment, becomes the place of redemption, and not a mere two-dimensional backdrop for the drama of individual salvation.

3. There is within the *Declaration* a remarkable challenge to some peculiarly evangelical attitudes to other people which are far from biblical. Put bluntly, embracing the truth that God is not only our Creator, but everyone's Creator, opens the way for us to renew our relationships with other people and find some level of true community in an increasingly fractured world. In A Rocha, we have come to call this wider fellowship the 'psychological community'. If we take our shared created identity, regardless of our beliefs, race, background and abilities, as the starting-point in understanding our relationship to other people, then we are aware of something in common that we share before God. If we take as our starting-point the fork where people may choose the broad or narrow road described by Christ, then there has been no relationship at all before we go our separate ways. Remember, by contrast, how Jesus related to the woman at the well in John 4, or how Paul speaks to the Athenians in Acts 17. That may do something to explain why so many people have first heard the Christian message as one of judgment or rejection. It may also explain why so many Christians are at a loss to relate normally to those who do not share their beliefs, and feel a burden of obligation to change such people, constructing artificial relationships with no sense of natural belonging together as human beings. The psychological community – the sense of fundamental belonging with others that comes from understanding we are created people first and Christians second – is in no sense a denial of the fact that God distinguishes between those who are his people and those who are not. But for us to *begin* with those distinctions, rather than with the prior recognition of God's creative love which brings all of us into being in the first place, is a distortion of the direction of biblical thinking. The *Declaration* affirms that we are 'shaped by the same processes and embedded in the same systems of physical, chemical and biological

interconnections which sustain other creatures'. Curiously, for many Christians it may be easier to accept our common place in creation with other creatures than our common place with other people! Yet as an idea it is theologically far less challenging. The 'us and them' habit, seen now in rising nationalism in Europe, and frequently found in the church in its understanding of how to relate to a society which doesn't believe in God, dies hard for us all.

We have sought to build those three elements into the way we live and work in A Rocha. Any organization trying to see practical progress in environmental work at the present time must live with a considerable degree of frustration. Those who need success in order to keep their supporters loyal, or to justify their work, are doubly under pressure. So the realization that what we do is first of all done as worship, as the simple recognition of God, can keep us sane. We are not bound to a tally of success, however hard we may work for what we believe to be right. And our understanding that redemption extends to every part of our lives and work, and that there is the possibility of redemption for the whole creation, continues to give us hope when we are faced with seemingly intractable practicalities. For A Rocha, these extend from the difficulties of securing legislation to protect a Portuguese wetland, to the endless complexities of obtaining a work permit for team members in Lebanon. Then of course there is never enough money for the task, which is maybe the area of human endeavour most resistant to redemption. But all this is the raw material of prayer, the place where our life in Christ is lived. Our endeavour is to work in a way that allows us to build genuine community with all comers, regardless of their beliefs. The commitment to Christ which is shared by those on A Rocha teams has never been seen as a barrier to anyone with appropriate skills being involved in the life of the centre or in the work of the group who are there. There is no secret agenda. Of course we want to share what we know of Christ, but we recognize fully that it must take place on the terms of a shared humanity.

So it may be that there is a considerable change ahead for those of us who remain firm in our commitment to the authority of Scripture, simply because we are firm in that commitment. There is an irony in the fact that it has been brought upon us, not by re-reading those Scriptures and acknowledging that our previous reading had undergone subconscious editing, but by the drastic events of our times. Ignoring our belief that creation is just as much God's revelation of his character to us as the

Scriptures themselves, too often we have been content to leave reflection on the world around us to theological liberals. But so dramatic is the destruction of creation that events have driven us back to Scripture for some kind of wisdom in the face of disaster. As we do so, we discover a rich heritage, and new departures which may lead us not only to a healing of our relationship with creation, but to a more biblical faith in God himself, the three-personed Creator, Redeemer and Sustainer of his creation.

There are always advantages and risks in coming afresh to Scripture. The familiar emphasis on individual sin led to a mistrust of God's goodness in creation. An overemphasis on creation may therefore be expected to mislead us about the depth of evil of which the human heart is capable. We will need a different kind of vigilance. I am grateful to Eugene Peterson for pointing me to P. T. Forsyth on prayer, in a passage which remains still pertinent some seventy years after it was originally written. Forsyth wrote:

> Prayer ... is the effectuation of all Nature, which comes home to roost there, and settles to its rest. It is the last word of all science, giving it contact with a reality which, as science alone, it cannot reach. And it is also the most practical thing in all man's action and history, as doing most to bring to pass the spiritual object for which all men and all things exist and strive.

If the *Declaration* provokes us to these things, it will not have been wasted.

15

Love your neighbour as yourself

Stephen Rand

Stephen Rand is the Prayer and Campaigns Director of The Evangelical Alliance Relief Fund (Tearfund).

'Teacher, which is the greatest commandment in the Law?'

Jesus replied: '"Love the Lord your God with all your heart and with all your soul and with all your mind." This is the first and greatest commandment. And the second is like it: "Love your neighbour as yourself."' (Matthew 22:36–37).

So there it is: surely these verses offer conclusive proof that concern for the environment is only an optional extra for the Christian. At best, it might be a suitable interest for the biology field-course enthusiast; at worst, it could reveal a theological woolliness verging dangerously on New Age freakishness. But at least we can be sure that if we wish to stick with the central concerns of Jesus, then we can safely leave the environment in the tender care of the vegetarian sandal brigade and give our own time to more pressing matters.

No! This view is not only sadly mistaken, but in fact dangerous for the cause of the gospel at this pivotal time in human history.

Empty observance

It has been difficult enough to persuade evangelical Christians that love for God cannot be separated from love for one's neighbour. In our own lives and teaching, we constantly have to fight the demonic tendency to replace living faith with dead religion. Religion is concerned with form, with ceremony, with ritual – and this is what we assume God requires of his worshippers. Or, to put it more provocatively: is it not significant that it is worship, in terms of style, instruments, merchandise and topic of conversation, that has perhaps become the major preoccupation of modern evangelicalism?

This internalized ecclesiasticism sits uneasily with the ferocity of the prophet Isaiah's declaration of God's rage at empty religious observance: 'Stop bringing meaningless offerings! Your incense is detestable to me. New Moons, Sabbaths and convocations – I cannot bear your evil assemblies' (Is.1:13). It contrasts sharply with the simple, direct words of Micah: 'And what does the LORD require of you? To act justly and to love mercy and to walk humbly with your God' (Mic. 6:8). It is not that there is anything wrong in seeking to give God the best we can in our worship. It is rather that God's priority is that our worship should inspire and reflect our desire to love God and to love our neighbour day by day, every day.

So, given the personal and corporate challenge involved in winning this battle, what greater battle is there in seeking to squeeze in even a morsel of concern for the environment? That is why I appreciate so much that this *Declaration* does not call us as evangelical Christians to some new agenda, or offer an optional extra for an *à la carte* theological menu; instead, it calls us back to consider once again the nature of God and the core of our faith. That is why these two simple yet profound verses in Isaiah and Micah offer a key to pursuing environmental issues and to discovering the heart of what it means 'to live in God's earth God's way'.

Living in God's creation

First, we are to love God with everything we have, and in every way we can. It is easy to forget that our understanding of God begins at the beginning: 'In the beginning, God created ...' It has become an important discipline for me in all my preaching on this topic to remember to emphasize that, when we talk about the environment we are not talking about a media topic, a private lobby-group interest, or a topical invention of the last few decades. We are talking about God's creation.

Christians are concerned about the environment, not primarily because of our concern for our children and the inheritance we hand on to them, but because of our concern for our Father and the inheritance that he has already handed on to us. We are not ashamed to stand up and proclaim that the Earth, far from being our mother, is the work of our Father. If God made it, it matters. If God made it to reveal his extraordinary creativity and lavish generosity, it deserves to be taken seriously. If God made it, and his Son's death and resurrection will allow it one day to be remade in all its full and intended glory, it can scarcely be regarded as a mere sideshow.

Yet many Christians still do not see this. One has to ask if they can imagine the pain of the parents who lovingly create a home for their children and one night return to find it wrecked by a teenage party, or simply treated as a hotel with a fridge to be raided and a place to dump dirty clothes; or of Michelangelo completing the Sistine Chapel ceiling and sharing all his learning, experience and skill with his children, then offering them the use of his paints for their own artistic expression – and finding that they have used them to scrawl ugly graffiti across his masterpiece.

If we want to enter into the experience of being the children of God, both in terms of rational awareness and emotional attachment, then in mind and heart we will know that the Father made the Earth, and he made it for us. The first commandment in Scripture – or perhaps we should see it as a call to the sharing of a privilege and responsibility – is to take care of it. If we are to love him with everything we have, how will we treat his masterpiece?

Tears for creation

I can still recall the day I saw a pastor cry. His tears were in such contrast to the scene of tranquil beauty that was ravishing my senses. It was a remote and inaccessible part of Honduras, deep in the largest remaining expanse of tropical rainforest in Central America. We were travelling in a dug-out canoe up the broad expanse of the Patuca River, the silent corridor of trees only occasionally disturbed by the lazy flight of a heron.

As we rounded a bend in the river, we came upon a scene of pastoral contentment as cows grazed solemnly and contentedly on the bank. But the Indian pastor wept, because when he had last travelled this way a few weeks earlier, the forest trees had extended to the water's edge. Now they had gone, despatched by a roaring chainsaw, sacrificed to the commercial greed of those eager to satisfy the world's insatiable appetite for burgers.

The pastor was not moved by a sentimental love of trees, or even a deep hatred of Western consumerism; he was a pastor, and his concern was for his flock. He explained that the cattle would come down to the bank to drink the water; the river bank would be eroded and the water polluted. The fish stocks would be affected – and his people depended on fish for their nutrition. The loss of the trees was a mark of the loss of their culture, their whole way of life.

The human race depends on the environment. And the human race means individual people, people made in the image of God, people for whom Christ died. It means Indian Christians who are part of the fellowship of the body of Christ. It means our neighbours, whom we are to love as ourselves.

The care of creation is love of our neighbour

Concern for the environment is inseparable from true and authentic love for our neighbours in two distinct and vital ways.

The first way is in recognizing, in the words of the *Declaration*, 'that human poverty is both a cause and a consequence of environmental degradation'. If we take seriously the words of Deuteronomy 15:4 that 'there should be no poor among you', whether we interpret this as a command or as a description of the result of obedience to God's law, then we will inevitably be concerned for those who live on the edges of society and who bear the brunt of environmental destruction. We read of global warming, then turn up the thermostat and drive to the supermarket, pondering the bewildering choice spread out before us. Meanwhile, millions build their homes on land vulnerable to flooding, work in an atmosphere filled with chemical pollution, or stare at the sky searching for the sign of rain that will bring life back to their land and to their families.

Tearfund is working in partnership with an indigenous Christian organization (MOPAWI) dedicated to the protection and development of the Indian peoples of the Mosquitia region of Honduras. Our concern is with the health and well-being of the people, old and young alike. In the Patuca River region, they face a land of continuing and rapid deforestation. Roads opened up by loggers offer easy access to landless labourers desperate to slash and burn in order to produce crops for their families; they also provide easy access for cattle barons looking for grazing. Both the trees and the fertility of the land are destroyed. But the Indians have no recognized legal title to the land which has sustained them for generations, no protection against the desperation and greed of the poor and wealthy outsiders. They face disaster.

And disaster has struck. Hurricane Mitch roared through Central America in November 1998. It brought torrential rain – and the deforested valleys, denuded of their natural protection against flash floods, became places of devastation as the rivers burst their banks and water levels reached unprecedented heights. The Patuca River valley was one of the worst affected. The Indians' livelihood was ruined; theoretical threat became awful reality.

I was in Ethiopia at the height of the famine crisis of the mid-1980s. The landscape was very different from that of Honduras. Parched, rocky ground gave testimony to prolonged drought, thought by many to be the result of climate change caused by deforestation. I remember the horror of famine: the sounds of awful wailing greeting the dawn as families woke to the loss of the weakest and most vulnerable; the unbelievably wasted limbs of the babies too far gone to be saved.

But I also remember Daniel. Daniel was a church leader, an evangelical Christian filled with a passion for the church to be at the forefront of change. The Ethiopian Kale Heywet (Word of Life) Church had persuaded the Marxist government of the time to give them 500 hectares of land. It was easy to see that the gift had not been generous. The area looked like a lunar landscape, bare, rocky, apparently useless. A dried-up ravine was the only sign of the river that had once run through the plot. The main road south from Addis Ababa crossed the site, people and animals trudging past, sometimes obscured by the dust stirred up by the occasional vehicle.

It looked hopeless. But Daniel had a vision of transformation. Local people had begun to terrace the land, and were being paid for their hard labour with food. Daniel proudly showed me the seedlings from the church's nursery that were planted along the edge of the terraces to hold the soil in place, to allow grazing to return for the animals, and to provide fruit and firewood in a managed forestry scheme. 'When these seedlings grow, and the land begins to be productive again,' said Daniel, 'then I will put up a sign by the roadside that will tell everyone who passes that the church is responsible.'

In 1992 Tearfund joined with Spring Harvest and British Youth for Christ in a major youth fundraising and education initiative, timed to coincide with the Rio Earth Summit. We called it *Whose Earth?* Every time these words were shouted by the leader, the young people yelled back, 'God's Earth!' We wanted to emphasize the simple point that it was the owner and Creator who called us to care for his creation.

The enthusiasm of the young people was encouraging, but not surprising: every survey showed that the environment was top of the list of their concerns for the future, for the planet. They were keen to do something about it, they were keen to raise money for the needs of the poor affected by it, they were willing to raise the money by being sponsored for carrying out a local act of creation care. It was 'Think global, act local' at its finest.

What quickly became clear was that, while these young people were deeply concerned about the environment, they had never heard anything about it in their churches. I recall meeting one twenty-year-old almost crying tears of joy because she had finally heard Christians talking about creation care. It was a startling example of both an age gap and a reality gap in the church. It highlighted for me the other way in which concern for the environment is inseparable from love for our neighbour.

The second way that we love our neighbour is by sharing the gospel of saving faith in Jesus Christ. Indeed, it is our love which motivates us to do this. The church is called to a holistic witness that includes both proclamation and demonstration of the good news that offers eternal life, life in all its fullness. Yet in failing to teach young people the relevant biblical truths that could build a truly Christian approach to the environment, the church has been closing the door on a vital route for the gospel. Its silence was – and is – a tragic missed opportunity of culturally relevant evangelism.

The church can offer more than silence. It can provide outright hostility. It can tarnish all talk of the environment by dubbing it part of a New Age plot, and leave young people convinced that the choice they face is between a concerned paganism and an uncaring Christianity. It is more than sad: it is unbiblical, and catastrophic in its effect.

At the time of *Whose Earth?* I answered the complaints letters that came in to Tearfund. We did not receive many. But I do remember one particularly vitriolic epistle that demanded to know why Tearfund was planting trees while people were going to a lost eternity. It was one of the times when I was glad to have met Daniel.

Three years after my visit to that rocky Ethiopian landscape, Daniel came into the Tearfund offices in Teddington. He told me about his project.

'You remember those six-inch seedlings I showed you?' he said. 'Now they are thirty feet tall!' The land had been transformed into a productive place once again; the Marxist government had been so impressed that the church had been given another 500 hectare plot.

He went on to explain that there had been another sign of God's work. His land was in a largely Muslim area of the country. Missionaries had preached for twenty years or so without noticeable effect. But now the local people were asking questions about why the church had come to work there, providing them with food in exchange for their labour, and creating an oasis of fruitfulness where there had previously been only desert. And Daniel was only too ready to tell them that it was because of God's love for them, a love that could not only see the landscape transformed, but a love that could transform their lives as well. As a result, some had made a commitment to Christ, and a church had been established. Planting trees had been persuasive preaching.

Sharing God's own concern for creation

Creation matters because God made it, God sustains it, and God will redeem it; if we love God with all we have, then we will share his concerns. The care of creation matters because our love for our neighbour around the world will encompass those who are vulnerable to the impact of environmental degradation. The care of creation matters because if we want people to hear the gospel, then we must allow them to see it loved and lived with an integrity and wholeness that demonstrate its relevance to their concerns as well as to their needs.

16

The *Declaration* in practice: missionary Earth-keeping

Susan Drake Emmerich

Susan Drake Emmerich was formerly employed in the US State Department, and while there she was involved in the negotiations both before and during the United Nations Conference on Environment and Development. More recently she has worked for the Au Sable Institute (p. 189), and has been instrumental in establishing its East Coast site, on an island in Chesapeake Bay.

The *Declaration* calls for followers of Jesus Christ 'to work for the *reconciliation* of all people in Christ, and to extend Christ's *healing to suffering creation* ... God's purpose in Christ is to *heal and bring to wholeness not only persons but the entire created order.* "For God was pleased to have all his fullness dwell in him, and through him to reconcile to himself all things, whether things on earth or things in heaven, by making peace through his blood shed on the cross"(Col. 1:19–20).'

The beginnings

This is the story of the three years I spent living on Tangier Island in Chesapeake Bay, on the eastern US seaboard. The island community was riven by conflicts within itself and with environmentalists seeking to help it cope with its falling resource base. I was interested in exploring the possibility of biblical stewardship principles being a means to resolving divisions between environmentalists and such a resource-dependent community, particularly one where the church was avowedly at the centre of the community's life. The hope was that they might provide a bridge between environmentalists and the islanders, and thence to a renewed harmony and justice for all those involved.

My starting-point was 'missionary Earth-keeping' as expounded by Calvin DeWitt and Ghillean Prance (1992): that which honestly acts upon a full understanding of creation, of its degradation, and of biblical principles for its proper care and keeping; an enterprise whose goal is the wholeness, integrity and renewal of people and creation and their relationships with each other and with the Creator.

DeWitt and Prance's work focused on cases where the missioner works in a foreign culture. The Tangier Island situation was different because I, a missioner, was working in a community within my own country, albeit in a very different culture from the one in which I grew up. The Tangier community, however, had economic and ecological parallels to those of many rural communities in the Two Thirds world.

The Tangier Island watermen community

Chesapeake Bay is the largest estuary in the United States; its watershed spans the states of New York, Virginia, Maryland, Pennsylvania and the District of Colombia. The bay supports numerous species of fish and crustaceans and provides an income for over 12,000 watermen and their families.

Tangier Island, Virginia, is a small archipelago in the middle of the bay, home to a unique watermen community of 650 people whose ancestors came from Cornwall, England, and who are descendants of the famous American explorer Davey Crockett. Because of its remote location, Tangier Island has been largely isolated for 200 years; the people still speak with an Elizabethan accent. 'Waterman' is an old English term still used in the Chesapeake Bay region to refer to one who harvests crabs and oysters. The church is the centre of community life and over 80% of the community consider themselves to be conservative evangelical Christians.

The Tangier Island population traditionally relied on collecting oysters and blue crabs, but because of damage to the oyster reefs from over-harvesting and from disease, the economy has become almost entirely dependent on a blue-crab fishery. Unfortunately this fishery also is now suffering from over-exploitation, compounded by pollution from farms and urban areas along the edge of the Chesapeake Bay. The decline in blue-crab yield has reduced the incomes of watermen and their families and created worries about their livelihood and way of life. This has prompted environmentalists to recommend stringent controls, which have aggravated underlying fears in the population, and surfaced in bitter conflict between watermen communities and environmental groups.

There are a host of environmental groups in the area, together with state and federal government agencies, recreational fishing groups and scientists. The largest environmental organization in the region is the Chesapeake Bay Foundation, devoted to 'saving the bay', and, as part of this, very much believing that the Chesapeake Bay region needs a thriving watermen community.

Discovering the causes of the conflict

To discover the true underlying causes of conflict between groups, it is necessary to identify the differences in ways people think, speak and act. Understanding people's worldview and their cultural language is especially important.

I lived and worked in and around the Tangier watermen community over a period of three years, spending many hours talking with watermen on their boats and out in crab shanties, and with women in the crab-processing houses. Conversation, as opposed to interviewing, is an art which has become marginalized in modern-day society. My conversations included discussions about what the people involved perceived to be the underlying causes of the conflict with the environmentalists, what role women and the church played in the community, and what were their views about the environment.

I unearthed a latent biblical environmental ethic within the community. Most watermen and women of faith believed there was a scriptural foundation to steward the environment and its creatures, including their catch species. This provided a bridge to help them understand and accept stewardship ideas promoted by the regional environmental group, which were otherwise regarded as threatening to the community. This was a crucial stage, with a Tangier Watermen's Stewardship Initiative being developed by the community.

The biblical principles of the Tangier environmental ethic which highlighted and provided the basis for the community-based Stewardship Initiative were:

- caretaking (godly stewarding of creation);
- maintaining the fruitfulness of the catch species;
- practising contentment;
- allowing for Sabbath rest for the creation;
- loving one's neighbour and hence not polluting the bay;
- obeying the law of God; and, therefore,
- obeying the civil laws, particularly those relating to the fishery laws.

These principles underlay a set of values which were jointly held by both the Christian watermen and the secular environmental groups. Once the environmentalists realized the need to accept the Tangiermen's faith framework, including language dealing with creation's care, a shared vision began to emerge.

The Tangier Watermen's Stewardship Initiative

My study revealed three important facts:

- the most pressing concern on the minds of the watermen was the threat to their existing way of life;
- there was a latent biblical environmental ethic within the community; and
- the major forces for change were the women and the church.

The women proved to have a better understanding than the men of the true causes for the conflicts within the community, and also a clearer vision for a possible economic and environmental future. They tended to have a broader perspective than the men, perhaps because they might have a husband in one part of the crab fishery, a father in another, and a son in yet another. This meant they had a stake in success for all fishermen and, therefore, a desire for fair regulations throughout the fishery. It was the women who saw the need to cooperate with environmentalists and scientists in order to ensure a healthy fishery. It also became clear, however, that if any change was going to take place in the community, it would have to come from or through the church.

With this background, I offered to return and assist the two island churches develop a biblically based stewardship initiative that would help them cope with the economic and environmental changes affecting them. This was welcomed by key leaders from both churches on the island. With full community participation, I worked within the biblical value system of the community and helped devise an environmental and economic stewardship initiative called 'The Tangier Watermen's Stewardship 2020 Vision'. The Initiative's leadership was entirely indigenous to Tangier Island and included the mayor, the pastors and lay leaders of both island churches, and the principal of the Tangier school. The Initiative was endorsed by the Town Council.

The next and defining event occurred at a joint service of both churches, when I preached on biblical environmental stewardship and loving one's neighbour. At that service, fifty-eight watermen bowed down in tears and asked God to forgive them for breaking the fishery laws. They then committed themselves to a Stewardship Covenant. This was a strange idea at first because the concept of a covenant, while firmly rooted in biblical theology, tends to be emphasized only in the Calvinist tradition. Notwithstanding, it had an immediate effect. From that time, many people's behaviour and attitudes changed both radically and positively towards the environmentalists on the island, towards the creation, and towards change for future. Watermen in their seventies and eighties, an age when habits tend to be fixed, began bringing their rubbish back to the island, rather than dumping everything overboard. Many apologized to fellow-Tangiermen working for the Chesapeake Bay Foundation, for their animosity over the years. Individuals spoke emotionally in church of their conviction of sin after throwing metal cans overboard or taking undersized crabs. Government officials, scientists and environmentalists, all of whom had experienced difficulty in instituting change of any sort, have been stunned by the dramatic change in the people of Tangier.

There is still opposition to the Stewardship Initiative. Opposition from family members and friends has been especially difficult, but it has had an important effect in causing those involved in the Stewardship Initiative to think through what they really understand the Scriptures to say about caring for creation and loving their neighbours. This has reinforced the thinking of those involved in the Initiative, producing strongly held convictions that there really is a sustainable and lasting future for their way of life.

Some oppose the Initiative because it is religious-based (although the Initiative has always been open to all people, and seven non-Christians took the covenant). Others object because they do not feel that one should need to make a covenant to obey secular laws. Still others dissent because they do not feel they can make a living without breaking the law, while others are simply suspicious of the covenant. Notwithstanding, more than half the islanders are in favour of the Stewardship Initiative, and only a small proportion adamantly oppose it.

In addition to the Watermen's Stewardship Covenant, the women have developed their own covenant, agreeing

1. to be better stewards of resources by consuming less;
2. not to give in to every desire of their children; and
3. to be less demanding on their husbands, who may be losing income due to their commitment to obey all the fishery laws.

A key goal of the Initiative was to empower people so that they could gain a sense of control over their environmental, economic and social destiny, based on a biblical value system. One outcome has been that the women are now organizing themselves, for the first time in the history of the island, into a political action group to work with government officials, environmentalists and scientists in order to fight for fair fishery regulations and fishery stewardship. They have become known as FAIITH (Families Actively Involved in Improving Tangier's Heritage) and provide a significant channel of communication between the watermen community and the Chesapeake Bay Foundation.

While not always agreeing with each other, some of the Tangier watermen and women are now working with the Foundation to restore the oyster reefs around Tangier, and to expand and diversify the local economy by developing oyster aquaculture. As a result of the 'revelation' about caring for creation, their neighbours and their economic future, watermen who despised oyster-farming a year ago are now trying out the new aquaculture technology around their crab shanties. At the same time, some of the women are considering whether to develop a craft-making co-op to help maintain the heritage of their culture through an income from tourism or a crabpot-making and boat-building enterprise.

A non-profit organization has been formed to implement the goals of the 2020 Stewardship Vision and to spread the biblically based stewardship and reconciliation message to other watermen and farming communities in the Chesapeake Bay catchment. Hopefully, the Tangier example of missionary Earth-keeping may provide the principles and a process relevant to other local resource-dependent communities even further afield.

Summary

The *Declaration*'s statements are not merely words, but reflect biblical truths that have stood the test of time. The *Declaration* calls on followers of Jesus Christ to work 'in the power of the Holy Spirit to share the Good News of Christ in word and deed, to work for the reconciliation of all people in Christ, and to extend Christ's healing to suffering creation'.

The Tangier Island experience involved healing and a renewed sense of harmony between people and the creation. It is a case study showing how biblical stewardship principles can provide a unique 'language' bridge between a secular environmental group and a resource-dependent, faith-based community.

For environmentalists, policymakers and scientists, events on Tangier have provided a pattern for understanding interactions within resource-dependent communities, including the importance of alternative forms of income, so that the community does not view caring for creation as 'jobs versus environment'. The Chesapeake Bay Foundation's acceptance of working within the Tangier community's faith-based system has helped open a channel of communication with the FAIITH group which has empowered women and disenfranchised watermen to take control of their economic and social future, by giving them a voice to talk with the environmentalists, scientists and government officials who create and implement the fishery regulations.

This faith-based approach should not be seen as a blueprint for all situations. Its methodology, however, may well be the basis for an organically developed approach by the native populations of other faith-based communities.

The *Declaration* states,

> The presence of the kingdom of God is marked not only by renewed fellowship with God, but also by renewed harmony and justice between people, and by renewed harmony and justice between people and the rest of the created world.

The sequence of events on Tangier shows that justice and harmony can spread throughout communities in environmental conflict because of the witness of Christ's power. It is a vivid example of Christ's power to change the lives of men and women involved in environmental conflict despite opposition from family and friends.

17

Population numbers and environmental degradation

John Guillebaud

John Guillebaud is Medical Director of the Margaret Pyke Centre of University College London, where he is Professor of Family Planning and Reproductive Health. He is a clinician, teacher, researcher and author of seven books plus 300 other publications on population, the environment, contraception and women's health issues.

Only one of the thirty-two 'bullet points' in the *Declaration* mentions population growth:

> Many of these degradations are signs that we are pressing against the finite limits God has set for creation. *With continued population growth*, these degradations will become more severe. Our responsibility is not only to bear and nurture children, but to nurture their home on earth [McMichael and Powles 1999]. We respect the institution of marriage as the way God has given to ensure *thoughtful procreation of children* and their nurture to the glory of God.

I was happy to sign the complete *Declaration*, since what was said was excellent. My sole concern relates to what was *not said* – what I saw as a serious 'sin of omission' located in the paragraph quoted above. The emphases are my own and I examine these two phrases below.

155

1. 'With continued population growth'

This phrase implies population growth as a *constant* to which we must adapt, rather than as something capable of being reduced to zero (with eventual stabilization of total human numbers) or even reversed (to achieve the eventual option of a stable, lower total number).

Unremitting population growth is impossible on a finite planet (Cohen 1995). The achievement of a decent life for those currently in degrading poverty depends on the global population being as little above the 1999 total of six billion as it can fairly and feasibly be. We will never meet human needs without stabilization of human numbers.

In declaring Christian solutions to the environmental crisis, the drafters of the *Declaration* have omitted one of the three critical factors from the 'IPAT' equation, as follows:

$$I = P \times A \times T$$

where:

I is the impact on the environment of a given society or civilization

P is the number of individuals in that society

A is their *per capita* affluence (with consequent 'effluence', linked to resource consumption *per capita*)

T is a composite factor accounting for the *per capita* impact of the technologies in use (however much they are reduced by 'greener' technologies, with lower energy use and maximum recycling of resources and potential pollutants)

It follows that efforts to reduce environmental damage by reductions in the *per capita* Affluence and Technology factors will be undermined if there are more and more 'capitas'. Brilliant success through green technology in halving pollution will be totally negated by a doubling of the number of pollu*ters*.

In many developing countries the **A** factor must increase, as a human right. That this increase in *per capita* disposable income involves some adverse effect on the local and global environment is something the 'haves' of the world must accept – and Christians should take a lead here. Recognizing that this makes global reduction in the **A**-factor even less probable and that there are strict scientific limits to the reductions possible in the **T**-factor, should not Christians therefore also have a view on reducing the **P**-factor?

Even without the environmental implications, there is a 'vicious circle'. Population increase causes more poverty, yet grinding poverty favours large family sizes and hence population increase (figure 1).

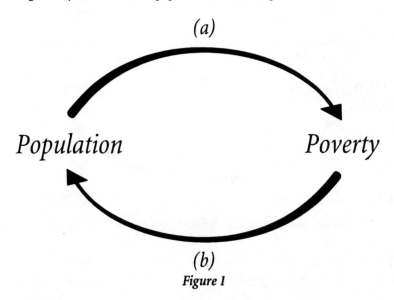

(a)

Population   *Poverty*

(b)

Figure 1

The vicious circle has two components: arrow (a) is created by the self-evident fact that if there are more humans in each generation, the finite 'cake' of a resource-poor country has to be divided among more and more individuals. Increasing the gross domestic product (GDP) is necessary (along with social justice, see below) to give a half-way decent life for all the inhabitants of that country. In many countries the increase in human numbers keeps on wiping out the gains, whether these be in agriculture, literacy or healthcare.

However, the second arrow (b) in figure 1 draws attention to another well-established fact: that, in situations of extreme poverty, reduction of family size appears disadvantageous: 'every mouth has two hands'. The labour of each new child in the family is welcomed, especially in the absence of social security for sickness and old age. High infant and child mortality also tends to reduce interest in birth-planning until a relatively high average family size is achieved.

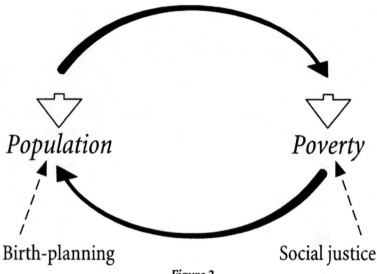

Figure 2

Yet, as shown in figure 2, the vicious circle can be transformed into a 'virtuous spiral', if we apply social justice and birth-planning with equal vehemence. This is what has occurred in recent times in countries as different as Thailand and Costa Rica. 'Social justice' includes many components, as highlighted at the 1994 World Population Conference in Cairo (Guillebaud 1995); they can be summarized in another slogan, 'Take care of the people and the population will take care of itself.' But such 'taking care' must include effective provision for voluntary birth-planning. We know from the the Demographic Health Surveys of 24,000 women in thirty-eight countries that it is untrue that most women in the South would not accept birth-planning (*Hopes and Realities* 1995; Guillebaud 1996). Regardless of however many children they already have, at least 50% of today's mothers in the most populous countries wish for no more children, but they often lack the methods. We are failing to push at an open door! Widespread availability of culturally appropriate family-planning services would greatly reduce maternal mortality (currently nearly 600,000 largely avoidable deaths per year as well as the worldwide tragedy of induced abortion, a method of fertility control which as Christians we reject. The hazard is that many people may subscribe to abortion and other coercive methods because there are too few voices that link family planning with social justice, and that argue the case for both with passion.

2. 'Thoughtful procreation of children': a Christian approach

Christians need to clarify their position on family planning within marriage, if only because many non-Christians think that Judeo-Christianity endorses pro-natalism *ad infinitum*. Most of the damage to God's creation in industrialized and non-industrialized countries is not so much wanton as inadvertent, because of competition from sheer numbers of humans leading to destruction of habitats for other species. If one looks at Genesis 1 it is striking that God instructed the plants and animals of the planet to be fruitful and multiply *before* that instruction was given to human beings. It is therefore, I believe, self-evident that the Creator did not, and does not, intend human beings to multiply so much that they prejudice the fruitfulness of so many other species in his wonderful creation (in the twentieth century, by orders of magnitude more than ever before). This would surely be contrary to his nature, because implicit in the whole Bible is an attribute of God which I would add to his omnipotence, his omniscience and his omnipresence; namely, his 'omni-common sense'. Even viewed solely from the standpoint of our own species, if obeying the instruction to 'multiply' leads to numbers which exceed the carrying capacity of the land available – and hence guarantee an increased number of deaths by starvation, disease or violence – this is hardly obeying God's instruction to 'be fruitful'!

We need to rediscover the two great commandments of Jesus (see Mark 12:29–31). I interpret these as follows. If we truly loved God, would we not wish to love and conserve what he has made? If your loved one makes something for you, do you not treasure it for ever? Indeed, this is explicitly stated at the first bullet point of the *Declaration* (see p. 18). However, the second great commandment is to love our neighbour as ourselves. If we truly loved our neighbour, then would we not more sacrificially (a) love our neighbour wherever he or she is, helping him or her to stabilize family numbers, and (b) love our future neighbour, which certainly requires us to ensure that there are not so many future neighbours that the planet becomes uninhabitable? We should work for quality of human life rather than quantity of human flesh (Bratton 1992).

Marriage was ordained because 'it is not good for the man to be alone ... For this reason a man will leave his father and mother and be united to his wife, and they will become one flesh' (Gen. 2:18, 24). God means this 'one-fleshness' to result from his gift of intercourse – a gift which is really a sacrament, an outward sign of a deep, inward commitment.

Some Christians believe that family planning, except by so-called natural methods, is always wrong; others that it is just permissible. I believe both groups are wrong. In my view, modern methods of birth control should be seen as a gift of God, both in helping many couples in their home lives, and in preventing a disaster of there being more people on the Earth than can live in harmony with God's creation.

An African Christian has said that the Christian home is meant to be like a re-creation (in a very imperfect way) of the original Garden of Eden: inhabited by a man and a woman who love God first and also love each other. He asks: what if their little Garden of Eden is in danger of destruction because of there being more children than this married Christian couple can properly care for?

Surely, birth-planning is right. It will allow the couple to fulfil God's great first purpose of marriage (the act that creates one flesh), without its second purpose of procreation eventually destroying their Garden of Eden.

18

Eschatology and hope

Ron Elsdon

Ron Elsdon is curate assistant of Ballymena in Northern Ireland. He has formerly worked as a professional geologist and with Crosslinks, an Anglican mission agency. His previous work on environmental issues includes Greenhouse Theology *(1992) and being a trustee of the A Rocha Centre in Southern Portugal.*

Christians are often uncomfortable with eschatology. This is not just because it is a big word; the whole concept causes problems. It conjures up pictures of extreme, or at least wacky, interpretations of the book of Revelation; of yet another Christian or quasi-Christian group announcing that the end of the world is coming tomorrow. So it is easy to overlook the fact that much of what is said in the New Testament about creation is to do with its eschatological destiny. This can be easily verified by consulting almost at random various articles on the care of creation by evangelical authors. The eschatological goal of creation tends either not to be mentioned, or at best to be incidental to the argument.

That being so, it is not surprising that eschatology tends to be ignored in environmental discussions. After all, the link with ethics seems obscure or even non-existent. This is especially the case when it comes to a Christian response to environmental problems, because (at least at first glance) eschatology seems to paint a picture of the annihilation of creation at the end of history: so why bother trying to save it now? The matter can be put in even starker terms (and I have had repeatedly to face this objection from Bible college students): if the end of history will involve the annihilation of creation, does not Christian involvement in green issues serve to delay the Lord's return?

In sharp contrast to this is the challenge issued by the *Declaration*:

> We encourage deeper reflection on the substantial biblical and
> theological teaching which speaks of God's work of redemption in
> terms of the renewal and completion of God's purpose in creation
> (see p. 21).

It may appear at first that this has little or nothing to do with caring for
creation *now*. Not only is it apparently to do with the end of history, but the
very terms 'reflection' and 'theological' could be taken to suggest that
nothing of present and practical value could emerge from such an exercise.

On the other hand, the inclusion of 'the renewal and completion of
God's purpose in creation' within the meaning of salvation and of
redemption points up quite clearly that creation and gospel cannot be
separated, as they often are in popular evangelical thought that owes too
much to Greek philosophy and not enough to Scripture (Elsdon 1992, esp.
chapter 8). The most obvious passage to cite is Romans 8:19–25; here it is
sufficient to note that Paul's vision of the goal of creation is where it
actually is – at the heart of his magnificent exposition of the Christian
gospel, rather than as an incidental comment tucked somewhere at the end
of the letter. As various commentators have pointed out, Paul is influenced
here by Old Testament texts, such as Genesis 3, which show how creation
was profoundly implicated in the fall of humankind, and his purpose in
this section of Romans is to show how Christ's ministry is to do with the
reversal of all that happened then (e.g. Moo 1996: 514, esp. note 34).

Of particular importance are the parallel statements in Colossians 1,
which state that Christ's death on the cross was to reconcile sinful human
beings to God (1:21), and to reconcile to himself 'all things' (1:20; Greek, *ta
panta*). P. T. O'Brien (1982: 56) comments on Colossians 1:20:

> ... heaven and earth have been brought back into their divinely
> created and determined order ... the universe is again under its
> head and cosmic peace has been restored.

But this throws the eschatological dimension (or, problem?) into
sharper relief: this is precisely what we do *not* see! Here we come face to
face with one of the problems that bedevilled the discussions on the care of
creation at the highly publicized 1991 Canberra conference of the World

Council of Churches. Colin Craston has recorded the tension between the theological statement that creation was reconciled to its Creator at the cross and the apparently more practical issue of caring for the planet; he notes that the lack of an eschatological dimension was criticized by conference delegates (Craston 1992).

Another feature of the Colossians 1 passage is of particular importance with regard to the eschatological goal of creation: namely, the fact of the Christ-centred nature of creation (1:15–17). As Colin Gunton points out, there is great appeal in 'optimistic, immanentist, progressive eschatologies' expounded by theologians such as Peacocke and Teilhard de Chardin, indebted as they are to the insights of cosmology and evolutionary biology. Yet, as Gunton also notes, they have little to do with the cross, or with the categories of sin and evil:

> ... the dynamic of evolution is not coterminous with the dynamic of the Spirit ... a theological account of creation must say that it has a destiny other than a continuing, if finite, progression to entropy and increasing complexity (Gunton 1991: 158).

He goes on to state:

> ... we are here engaged not merely in a dialogue between science and theology, but in an encounter between what makes for life and what for death. Ontology and ethics, creation and redemption, cannot be treated apart from one another (1991: 159).

I agree with Gunton when he here implies that eschatology has ethical consequences, even though it might not seem obvious at first that the prospect of the Lord's return and the end of history can help us very much in making responsible environmental choices today or tomorrow. Yet the link between eschatology and ethics needs to be explored further, because throughout the New Testament this link is quite evident.

There are two examples in 1 Corinthians.

First, in 1 Corinthians 1:4–7, where Paul begins to address the moral and doctrinal confusion rampant in the church at Corinth, he refers to the abundance of their spiritual gifts (one of the major factors in the problem): 'Therefore you do not lack any spiritual gift as you eagerly wait for our Lord Jesus Christ to be revealed' (1:7). Secondly, in the sustained exposition of the resurrection and the eschatological hope of the resurrection body in 1 Corinthians 15, Paul concludes with a strong ethical imperative: 'Therefore, my dear brothers, stand firm. Let nothing move you. Always give yourselves fully to the work of the Lord, because you know that your labour in the Lord is not in vain' (15:58).

This brings us back to the issue we began with: namely, the fact that modern Christians are often uncomfortable with eschatology, and that ethics are seldom addressed in eschatological terms. I will now proceed to explore this link briefly in two ways.

1. Jürgen Moltmann's theology of hope

It has often been pointed out that the German theologian Jürgen Moltmann has been particularly important in restoring the eschatological dimension of Christian theology to its central place in mainstream Christian thought.[1] Moltmann starts with the apparent contradiction between the cross and resurrection: one is to do with God-forsakenness, the other with the nearness of God. The resurrection is, for Moltmann, the *contradiction* between what reality is presently like, and what God promises that it will one day be.

Further, the contradiction is centred on the person of Jesus as the crucified and risen one. This means that what lies in the promise and purpose of God beyond the end of history is not for a world which is totally unrelated to this one, but for the new creation of this world. It is only then that the promise inherent in the resurrection will be completely fulfilled.

In Moltmann's exposition of resurrection and eschatology, the promise is related to the present:

> The promise reveals the world to be transformable in the direction of its promised future, and so it rouses active hope which seeks out possibilities of change and creates anticipations of the future kingdom of God. This hopeful activity is the church's task in the world (see Bauckham 1993: 386).

There is, in Moltmann's work, food for considerable reflection on engagement with practical issues of environmental care. This is especially so given the observations by Craston, mentioned earlier (p. 162), of the World Council of Churches' statement on Justice, Peace and the Integrity of

Creation. In the light of the prayer, 'Come, Holy Spirit – renew the whole creation', he asks: 'In what way, if at all, does the present planet and all that is on it, and indeed the universe as we perceive it, partake of this new creation?' (Craston 1992: 36). Twice in his article in *Anvil*, Craston suggests that the idea of 'preservation might be better than that of renewal' (1992: 35–36), and he may be echoing a sentiment that others share: there is very little visible evidence that the situation of our planet is moving the way of the eschatological purpose of God.

It is here that Moltmann's theology of hope, and the biblical material that undergirds it, address the pragmatism that informs popular 'concern' for the environment. It is often addressed in such a way as to suggest that a few simple and painless measures such as regular trips to the bottle bank will solve all our problems. Linked with this is the expectation that problems can always be turned around in a relatively short space of time.

As with other global problems of our time, there are no easy or short-term solutions: they will have to be costly, and applied over a long period of time, in order to reverse the effects of large-scale processes and trends that have been operative over decades or even centuries. It is only the eschatological dimension of Christian hope that can nurture the theological understanding that is necessary if Christians themselves are to be meaningfully engaged over the length of time needed (rather than simply jump from one fad to the next).

2. Christian hope and environmental care

The conviction that God's promises will finally be fulfilled will also help Christians confront another dimension of environmental action: that of the pain of caring for a defaced and corrupted creation. This was the effect on many people of seeing pictures of seabirds coated in oil after Saddam Hussein's army attempted to sabotage Kuwaiti oil wells at the end of the 1991 Gulf War. After he had surveyed one stretch of polluted seashore, RSPCA officer Tim Thomas declared: 'This is the worst oil disaster I have ever seen. As I walked the beaches I came across a dead bird every two or three paces. They were just blobs of oil. I saw birds diving into the black water and never coming up. It was horrific' (quoted in Elsdon 1992: 104).

However misguided members of organizations such as the Animal Liberation Front may appear to be, they are often people who do share the pain of a suffering creation. The 1991 Gulf War is only one example: there are many others. It is not only animals and birds which suffer, however. The United Nations now recognizes the existence of *environmental refugees*. There are hundreds of millions of such, forced from their homeland, usually rural, by various kinds of environmental disaster, and often seeking some pathetic kind of security in the shanty towns of many of the world's mega-cities.

Faced with problems on such a large scale, despair comes easily, especially after the compassion fatigue induced by a decade or more of harrowing TV pictures and relief-agency advertisements. The awareness of the eschatological hope is *confident*: it is worth working for the renewal of creation now because of our confidence in what the sovereign Creator has revealed to us – both in the Scriptures and in the work of Christ himself – about the glorious future that awaits not only the children of God, but also creation itself.

This hope is, at the same time, *realistic*: it recognizes that creation will continue to groan until the appointed end of history, and therefore we must expect our efforts to be only partial, and their fruits to be hard-won.

19

The spirit of environmentalism

Michael S. Northcott

Michael S. Northcott teaches at New College, University of Edinburgh. He is author of an important study, The Environment and Christian Ethics *(1996) and more recently* Life After Debt *(1999).*

When the *Declaration* was first launched in the United States in 1994, Ronald Sider, one of its principal sponsors, identified an underlying motive as follows:

> One of the important things is that there are environmentalists out there who are saying some very crazy things, in terms of religion and theology. They're New Age, they worship the earth, mother goddess, and so on. And at the same time it's important to realize that they're groping for spiritual meaning, they're groping for a religious foundation, but they don't think Christianity is the way to get it (quoted in Beisner 1997:9).

Unlike many conservative Christians who see Earth-worship as evidence of the irredeemably pagan character of the environmental movement, Sider sees Earth-worship as a manifestation of a spiritual yearning among environmentalists, and a recognition of the ultimately spiritual character of the environmental crisis. He proposes that the spiritual quest represented by modern environmentalism can be truly fulfilled only through using 'biblical truth' as the 'foundation that we need for working seriously at our environmental problems' (quoted in Beisner 1997: 9).

When we turn to the *Declaration* we find that, in its opening paragraph, it seems to address precisely the trinity of concerns that Sider identifies: worship and spirituality, biblical truth, and environmental problems: 'because we worship and honour the Creator, we seek to cherish and care for the creation'. In other words, right attitudes to creation, which can generate care for creation, rather than abuse, are linked to truthful and spiritual worship of the Lord of Creation. Further attention is given to these concerns in the third section, which commences with an acknowledgment that 'many concerned people are convinced that environmental problems are more spiritual than technological'.

However, this clear connection between spiritual and environmental problems is not followed through in the *Declaration*'s account of the responses to environmental problems which the Bible calls Christians to make. Christians are to 'repent of attitudes which devalue creation', they are to root their actions in the revelation of Christ in the Scriptures, to learn from the Bible about the Creator, creation and the human task, and to learn from creation about God's divinity and the God-given order of the Earth. The primary emphasis of these responses is not spiritual, or even ethical, but rational and propositional. The underlying assumption seems to be that, provided we have true knowledge of God, and of the doctrine of creation, we will acquire the right attitudes so that we will act ethically in our treatment of creation.

While the *Declaration* seems to support the judgment of many environmentalists that the environmental crisis represents a spiritual problem, most of the actual text of the *Declaration* subordinates worship and spirituality to the affirmation of principles of biblical faith, and to education in the truth about God and creation. Where worship is referred to, it is primarily of an intellectual kind – a 'change of attitude'.

But worship, true and false, is at the heart of our ecological crisis. It is precisely the modern devotion to the cult of consumerism which is driving the horrific global scale of environmental destruction. The modern Western appetite for a constant and changing flow of consumer goods represents a spiritual disease, and is indicative that Western civilization has at its heart a devotion to that which is not God. 'Idolatry' is the word used in the Old Testament to describe the worship of created things in the place of God. And idolatry is wrong, not only because it displaces the worship of God with the worship of that which is not God, but also because the worship of these non-gods, or idols, is itself a source of evil. The gods of the Egyptians and the Babylonians required human sacrifice and legitimated slavery. These 'non-gods' did not partake of the righteousness of God and, in worshipping them, the people of Israel themselves abandoned the righteousness and justice of God. An idolatrous society is a society where injustice and oppression thrive and the laws of God are forgotten.

Idolatry, unrighteousness and injustice do not only have implications for human society. They also generate problems in the environment, as rulers and landlords abuse the land in the pursuit of human greed, war and domination. Hence the Old Testament writers associated true worship with the preservation of the land, just as they argued that idolatry was the cause of ecological destruction. As the Deuteronomist says:

> I have set before you today life and prosperity, death and destruction. For I command you today to love the LORD your God, to walk in his ways, and to keep his commandments, decrees and laws; then you will live and increase, and the LORD your God will bless you in the land (Deut. 30:15–16).

The Ten Commandments established this fundamental connection between worship and ethics, including the ethical treatment of created things. The first commandment states that 'You shall have no other gods before me. You shall not make for yourself an idol in the form of anything in heaven above or on the earth beneath' (Exod. 20:3–4). Following this commandment concerning true worship are two more on the same theme, one concerning the veneration of the name of the Lord, which is stated negatively as 'You shall not misuse the name of the LORD your God' (Exod. 20:7), and the other concerning Sabbath-keeping: 'Six days you shall labour and do all your work, but the seventh day is a Sabbath to the LORD your God' (Exod. 20:9–10). On the foundation of three commandments which establish the conditions for the performance of true worship of the Lord are set the remaining commandments, concerning respect for persons (not murdering, not lying, not committing adultery) and for all other created things (not stealing and not coveting).

In the Commandments, as in the whole pattern of Earth-keeping commended in the Bible, the just and holy treatment of creation is predicated on the priority given to the worship and the love of God among the people of God. From right worship, and right relationship to God, flows the recognition that 'the earth is the LORD's' (Ps. 24:1). So too does the recognition that the Lord has established limits on the human use and appropriation of the riches of creation, as exemplified in the Sabbath and Jubilee laws, which restrain human work on the land, and which prescribe periodic redistribution of nature's wealth between rich and poor.

The connection between right worship and the right and ethical use of nature in the Old Testament is allied with another equally important connection between right worship, the practice of the justice of God (*sedeq*), and the fertility and harmony of nature itself. In Psalm 72 the fertility of the land is said to be related to the expression of divine justice in the rule of King Solomon:

> He will judge your people in righteousness,
>   your afflicted ones with justice.
> The mountains will bring prosperity to the people,
>   the hills the fruit of righteousness.
> He will be like rain falling on a mown field,
>   like showers watering the earth.
>
> (Ps. 72:2–3, 6)

And the prophets made a similar connection in reverse:

> But these people have stubborn and rebellious hearts;
>   they have turned aside and gone away.
> They do not say to themselves,
>   'Let us fear the LORD our God,
> who gives autumn and spring rains in season,
>   who assures us of the regular weeks of harvest.'
> Your wrongdoings have kept these away;
>   your sins have deprived you of good.
>
> (Jer. 5:23–25)

Jeremiah identifies the diminishing fertility of the fragile soils of the promised land with the idolatry of the people of Israel who abandoned the true worship, and the right judgment, of Yahweh. Similarly, Isaiah argues that the declining fertility of Israel's crops and vineyards is a consequence of their neglect of divine laws restraining the wealthy and upholding the claims of the poor:

> Woe to you who add house to house
>> and join field to field
> till no space is left
>> and you live alone in the land.

The LORD Almighty has declared in my hearing:

> Surely the great houses will become desolate,
>> the fine mansions left without occupants.
> A ten-acre vineyard will produce only a bath of wine,
>> a homer of seed only an ephah of grain.

(Is. 5:8–10)

What we find here is an ancient Israelite recognition of a moral law which is set into the created order, a natural law which connects the fecundity of the land with the performance of righteousness in both worship and ethics, according to the covenant made between the Creator and the people of Israel (Northcott 1996). This moral law expresses a dynamic relationship between the worship of God and the harmony of created order, and between social justice and ecological harmony. This relationship is also reflected in the wisdom literature, including Proverbs and Ecclesiastes, where natural wisdom in the providential ordering of creation is said to find expression in the instincts and practices of animals, birds and insects, a wisdom which humans are said to ignore at their own, and nature's, peril.

The connection between human injustice and ecological breakdown is now well established in environmental history. The *Declaration* itself acknowledges this connection when it suggests that poverty, as well as being a cause of environmental degradation, is also, and often, a consequence of it. But, viewed in the light of the Old Testament linkage between human injustice and environmental breakdown, the pursuit of ecological justice is a spiritual and not just a social project. Analogously, in the light of the recognition in the Old Testament of the spiritual significance of limits on human work and exchange activity, the contradiction between an exponentially expanding economy of money and the finite resources of the economy of nature, which money transforms into productive capital, has a spiritual as well as an economic significance. In this perspective, reordering the economy towards sustainability, and restraining our participation in the 'allure of ... overconsumption', as the *Declaration* rightly suggests we must, are also and again spiritual works, and not just social acts.

The problem with the *Declaration* is that, despite its affirmations of the need for behavioural change, its authors understate the genuine spiritual work which such change involves. By contrast, many environmentalists, and particularly 'deep ecologists' such as Arne Naess, have long maintained that wasteful and ecologically rapacious consumerism is a manifestation of a deep spiritual malaise in modern individuals and societies. Environmentalists such as Naess argue that, instead of looking for self-fulfilment through consumerism, modern humans need to find their spiritual fulfilment through an engagement with nature, and especially wilderness. In the peak experiences, the pain and the joy which mountain-hiking or wilderness-walking can bring, humans can find an experience of self-transcendence which displaces the meaning vacuum which so many modern people seek to fill by the consumption of things (Naess 1989).

Naess's ecological philosophy, with its strong emphasis on nature experience, is precisely the kind of philosophy which the *Declaration* is intended to address with biblical truth. But because of the overemphasis on doctrinal and revelational truth at the expense of spiritual and ethical performance, the document does not present a convincing theological and spiritual alternative to the nature-spiritualism of many modern environmentalists.

From a biblical perspective, there can be no question that identification with wilderness, and the peak experiences that Naess speaks of, are alone unlikely to produce the profound spiritual reorientation of modern human society which is needed if we are to begin to live within the ecological limits of the planet. Nor are they a sufficient response to the source of the problem, which is not consumerism *per se* but the displacement, which consumerism reflects and enhances, of the orientation of human life towards God, and the corrosion of those virtues, such as love, justice, prudence and fidelity, which are essential to the practices of sustainable living and ecological justice (see, for example, Nash 1992). In Christian tradition, this orientation is stirred up, and these virtues are sustained, in worshipping communities wherein the performance of praise and worship draws people towards the love of God, and strengthens individuals and the community in lifestyles which express the spiritual fruits – or virtues – which characterize Christian living.

The performative significance of praise and worship – their capacity to change the participants both spiritually and morally – is given particular biblical emphasis in the Psalms, which record the power of praise to transform infidelity into faithfulness, and greed and lust into generosity and love, in the lives of the ancient Israelites. According to the psalmist, praise is the fundamental spiritual posture of the creation towards the Creator, and it is in the voice of praise and worship that he vividly evokes the spiritual unity between humans and nature:

> ... you mountains and all hills,
>   fruit trees and all cedars,
> wild animals and all cattle,
>   small creatures and flying birds,
> kings of the earth and all nations,
>   you princes and all rulers on earth,
> young men and maidens,
>   old men and children.
>
> Let them praise the name of the LORD.
> (Ps. 148:9–13)

The psalmist in these words expresses a sense of the spiritual unity between humans and the natural world which speaks more powerfully to the 'spiritual yearning' of many modern Earth-worshippers than the propositional approach to biblical truth which the *Declaration* manifests. The psalmist also expresses the ecological significance of worship of the Creator in this image of praise as a form of being which is not limited to the human but is writ large in the wondrous diversity and glorious music of all created life.

The *Declaration* is a welcome sign of the greening of evangelicalism in both North America and Britain. In the USA, far more than in Britain, it requires a considerable degree of courage for evangelicals to pen and publicly to affirm such a document, because so many conservative Christians in the United States regard environmentalism as both a betrayal of the American dream of liberty and prosperity, and a pagan subversion of true, biblical Christianity. The USA is a country which is in denial about the environmental crisis, and in particular about global warming, as witness the price of petrol at the pump, which is still below one dollar per gallon. Despite the strong consensus amongst scientists around the world that profligate energy consumption in modern industrial societies is primarily responsible for climate change today (p. 125), the United States media constantly regale the car-addicted American public with putatively scholarly refutations of the human role in climate change, while United States politicians have been vociferous in their opposition to significant reductions in energy consumption at international environmental gatherings such as those held in Rio de Janeiro and Kyoto.

The *Declaration* would, however, have made a stronger, and a more *biblical*, case had it identified the modern substitution of the idols of consumerism for the worship of God as the fundamental theological and spiritual challenge posed by environmental crisis. In challenging the eco-logically rapacious religion of consumerism, affluent Western Christians need to become more conscious, as their brothers and sisters in the southern hemisphere more often are, of the biblical claim that true fulfilment and true joy are not found in the quality or quantity of people's possessions but in the quality of their relationships – with God, with one another and with all creation. Fidelity and love towards God, expressed in spiritual worship of the Lord of creation, and in local communities of faith which express care for particular *places* on God's Earth, are the most powerful means which Christians can offer to unseat the ecologically rapacious practices of the modern idolatry of consumerism, and to challenge the false prophets of Earth-worship (Northcott 1996: 308ff.).

Part IV
Conclusions

The Bible has a deceptively simple and clear-cut concept of creation care.

1. The Earth belongs to God (Ps. 24:1) by his creation (Job 38:4; Ps. 19:1), sustaining (Matt. 6:26), redemption (Col. 1:15–30), and power to destroy (Gen. 6:7; Ps. 104:29); it is the theatre of his work (Gen. 9:12–17; Hos. 2:21–22; Matt. 5:45). Creation is 'good' and intrinsically valuable (Gen. 1:31; Job 38 – 41; Ps. 148:1–10; Matt. 10:29); it is separate from God (Gen. 2:20), connected to him by his word (Gen. 1:3, 6, 9, etc.; John 1:1–5; Heb. 1:3) and saved from reification by the incarnation (Mark. 4:41; Eph. 1:22; Phil. 2:10–11).

2. God has entrusted his creation to us as his managers (Gen. 1:26; Ps. 8:6–8) or gardeners (Gen. 2:15). We are answerable to him for his trust (Lev. 25:3–5, 14–17; Luke 12:42–48; 19:12–27; 20:9–18), not as preservationists but as responsible stewards (Matt. 25:24–30).

Our relationship with creation has been disrupted by the events described in Genesis 3:1–7, which we call the 'fall'. The fall is a specifically Christian doctrine; it is not directly referred to in other parts of the Old Testament, and plays little part in the rabbinic or Jewish apocalyptic tradition (P. E. Colwell in Ferguson and Wright 1988: 249; see also Wenham 1987; Dunn 1988). The Christian understanding is based almost wholly on chapters 5 and 8 of Romans and chapter 15 of 1 Corinthians.

The key passage for interpreting the effect of the fall on the non-human creation is in Romans 8:

The created universe is waiting with eager expectation for God's sons to be revealed. It was made subject to frustration, not of its own choice but by the will of him who subjected it, yet with the hope that the universe itself is to be freed from the shackles of mortality and is to enter upon the glorious liberty of the children of God. Up to the present, as we know, the whole created universe in all its parts groans as if in the pangs of childbirth (Rom. 8:19–22, REB).

This is a difficult passage. Most expositors do not help much. Handley Moule says, 'Among the many explanations of its meaning, two are the most representative and important. Of these (A) takes the passage to refer to the vague but deep longings of mankind for a better future; (B) to the longings, in a certain sense of "creation" as distinguished from man, for a coming glory' (1879: 149). Martyn Lloyd-Jones (1975) seems to regard it as wholly apocalyptic. James Dunn comments:

The point Paul is presumably making, through somewhat obscure language, is that God followed the logic of his proposed subjecting of creation to man by subjecting it yet further in consequence of man's fall, so that it might serve as an appropriate context for fallen man: a futile world to engage the futile mind of man ... There is an out-of-sortness, a disjointedness about the created order which makes it a suitable habitation for man at odds with his creator (1988: 487).

But what is this 'disjointedness' in creation? Blocher points out that while Paul

... declares that the whole created order has been subjected to vanity because of Adam – for the fall of the head had repercussions over the whole domain entrusted to him ... he gives no indication of either the extent or, above all, the form of the change. The Psalms which sing of God's creation as we now see it and the texts in the book of Job which celebrate its awesome beauty stand as a warning against the temptation to exaggerate the difference for nature itself (1984: 183).

In his commentary on Genesis, Derek Kidner refers directly to the

Romans passage in a way that links the pre-fall situation with our present existence: 'Leaderless, the choir of creation can only grind on in discord. It seems, indeed, from Romans 8:19–23 and from what is known of the pre-human world, that there was a state of travail in nature from the first, which man was empowered to "subdue" ... until he relapsed instead into disorder himself' (1967: 73). Rothschild and Martin (1993) have documented cases of disease in fossilized animals from times before the creation of humans.

Charles Cranfield has powerfully extended the same idea with an argument which shows the absurdity of attributing emotion to non-living things:

> What sense can there be in saying that 'the sub-human creation – the Jungfrau, for example, or the Matterhorn, or the planet Venus – suffers frustration by being prevented from properly fulfilling the purpose of its existence?' The answer must surely be that the whole magnificent theatre of the universe, together with all its splendid properties and all its life, created for God's glory, is cheated of its true fulfilment so long as man, the chief actor in the great drama of God's praise, fails to contribute his rational part. The Jungfrau and the Matterhorn and the planet Venus and all living things too, man alone excepted, do indeed glorify God in their own ways; but, since their praise is destined to be not a collection of individual offerings but part of a magnificent whole, the united praise of the whole creation, they are prevented from being fully that which they were created to be, so long as man's part is missing, just as all the other players in a concerto would be frustrated of their purpose if the soloist were to fail to play his part (1974: 227).

Blocher makes essentially the same point: 'If man obeys God, he would be the means of blessing to the earth; but in his insatiable greed ... and in his short-sighted selfishness, he pollutes and destroys it. He turns a garden into a desert (cf. Rev. 11:18). That is the main thrust of the curse of Genesis 3' (1984: 184).

The fall is a way of describing the fracture in relationship between God and the human creature made in God's image. C. F. D. Moule comments that Romans 8:19–22 means 'that man is responsible before God for nature. As long as man refuses to play the part assigned him by God, so long the entire world of nature is frustrated and dislocated. It is only when man is fitting into his proper position as a son in relation to God his Father that the dislocation in the whole of nature will be reduced' (1964: 12).

This is the message underlying the *Declaration*. We cannot blame our environmental degradation on God's 'curse' on the soil, or hide ourselves behind a claim that we are merely one species among many, implying with McHarg and Nicholson (pp. 26–27) that all will be well once we forswear the role given to us by God. Indeed, a balancing act in the debate about anthropocentrism versus biocentrism is not one for the Christian. The biblical position is unequivocal: we are called to be theocentric anthropocentrists, worshipping the Creator with the whole created order and exercising our proper function as God's caring agents. 'Man who is no longer responsible is not man whom God intended' (Westermann 1971: 97).

However, we need to beware of the hubris of expecting creation to depend on our care for it. God has created the Earth with its own properties and limits, and learning how to work with and within these is a major task of the scientific enterprise, far removed from the search for technological domination rightly condemned by some contributions to this commentary. The need for a better understanding of the Earth's Sabbaths is relevant here. John Polkinghorne believes that 'Natural theology is currently undergoing a revival, not so much at the hand of the theologians (whose nerve, with some honourable exceptions, has not yet returned) but at the hand of the scientists' (1988: 15). Although it is both inappropriate and dangerous to seek moral lessons from nature,[1] one of the reasons why the *Declaration* is necessary is that there are inbuilt constraints in the way we treat creation, including our attitudes to our fellow-creatures. Although we should properly worship the Creator through his works and acknowledge his authorship of the 'book of nature' (Acts 14:17; Rom. 1:20; Heb. 11:3), we must also read his 'book of words' (i.e. the Bible) if we are to discover his will in anything approaching a balanced way.

The Bible is unequivocal that the present world order will end with the return of God into world history. However it is also explicit that the judge of the world will be none other than the Saviour (e.g. Rev. 1:17–18). Romans 8:21, which is part of the key to a robust theology of creation, clearly speaks of renewal rather than replacement. Even such verses as 2 Peter 3:10 ('The day of the Lord will come like a thief. On that day the heavens will disappear with a great rushing sound, the elements will be dissolved in flames, and the earth with all that is in it will be brought to judgement', REB) need not be interpreted to mean the end of this present creation – particularly since the context emphasizes the scrutiny of human deeds rather than annihilation, consistent with other passages about the refining effects of fire. Although there will always be those who insist that the present dispensation is temporary and hence dispensable, the weight of Scripture is that 'this earth is precious to God and proper stewardship of non-human nature is a task with eternal consequences' (Finger 1998).

Creation care cannot be written off as a minority enthusiasm. The contributors to this book and many others (e.g. Fowler 1995; Bouma-Prediger 1995; Fergusson 1998; Berry 1999) show that it has become a concern of major theologians. No longer do Christians have to rely on secular analyses, good though many of these are; no longer do Christians have to defend themselves against the attacks of unbelievers (e.g. Nicholson 1987; Suzuki 1997); no longer do conservative Christians have to shrink from contentious or dubious theology (such as process thought or extreme liberalism; e.g. Birch et al. 1998; Dowd 1991) or even their extreme right-wing colleagues (Whelan, Kirwan and Haffner 1996; Beisner 1997; O'Hear 1997).

There are plenty of unresolved problems about creation, many of long standing. The question of the 'last things' has already been mentioned. Then there is the interpretation about the 'goodness' and 'completeness' of God's work. Traditionally, the world and its creatures were seen to be literally 'good ... very good', since, when 'God brought to an end all the work he had been doing ... he finished all his work of creation' (Gen. 2:2–3, REB). This simple – and effectively deist – understanding became stretched when the age of the Earth began to be better discerned in the eighteenth and nineteenth centuries, coupled with the growing realization that there had been changes in the structure and inhabitants of creation in times before humans appeared (i.e. before Noah's flood). William Buckland (1837) faced up to this in his Bridgewater Treatise, and argued that animal death should be distinguished from human death; the former is part of the Creator's provision for his creation, whilst the latter entered the world through Adam's disobedience (Rom. 5:12). Buckland was forced to this conclusion, not by any speculation about evolutionary ideas, but because he was faced with the inexorable evidence for a long Earth history. This proved to be the death-blow to deistic natural theology[2] and ironically opened the way for evolution to become theologically important – if God was Creator, he had to be seen as overseeing and 'holding all things together', i.e. fully immanent as well as wholly transcendent (Moore 1889: 73).[3]

Despite the signs of apparent 'cruelty' and 'waste' in 'nature, red in tooth and claw', men and women from the psalmists onwards have found awe and wonder and praise in their contemplation of creation. From a secular point of view, Bryan Norton (1987) has highlighted the 'transformative' value of nature, that is, the effect on individuals (and communities) of exposure to nature, an interaction which produces change distinct from the narrow instrumental worth with which economists value creation. A number of commentators in this volume call our attention to the worship to which we are called through and with creation. They remind us that stewardship is only part of our response to God's mandate. This is a New Testament truth as well as an Old Testament emphasis. As Jürgen Moltmann (p. 109) says: 'whoever reverences Christ also reverences all creatures in him; Christ is in everything created'. And Richard Bauckham, Oliver O'Donovan and Michael Northcott all point us beyond the role of the Word in creation to the Word made flesh.

This leads to two final points. As Christians we can and should make common cause with others in the care of creation, not least because the Genesis commands to have dominion and to tend the garden were given to all human beings at our birth as men and women in God's image. But, although we may share the pragmatism and self-interest of the world, it is not enough. Nor is it enough to be ever more assiduous gardeners, as Richard Bauckham points out (p. 103). The criticism that stewardship is an unhelpful concept, because it implies an entailed employee working for an absent landlord, would be true, if that is all that creation care means (e.g. Palmer 1992). The answer to the critics is to point out that stewarding is only part of our role; our God-given purpose is worship of the Creator in the company of all created beings (not merely as human beings sometimes meeting in church). God's covenant is with us as creatures in his image; and not only that, but also 'with every living creature' (Gen. 9:10). We share our stewardship with our fellow-human beings (whether or not they acknowledge the Creator); we add to their work a recognition and acknowledgment that our work is part of our commitment and worship of the one who made us in his own image, who is Creator of all, and who has reconciled 'all things' to himself through Christ's death on the cross (Col. 1:20; see Hall 1986). As Jürgen Moltmann (p. 110) reminds us, we are part of a cosmic process. In Oliver O'Donovan's words:

> The redemption of the world, and of mankind, does not serve only
> to put us back into the Garden of Eden where we began. It leads us
> on to that future destiny to which, even in the Garden of Eden, we
> were already directed. For creation was given to us with its own goal
> and purpose, so that the outcome of the world's story cannot be a
> cyclical return to the beginnings, but must fulfil that purpose in the
> freeing of creation from its 'futility' (O'Donovan 1986: 55).

This places the *Declaration* as indisputably 'evangelical', because it
proclaims truly 'good news'. The adjective is backed by John Stott's
definition of 'evangelical' as incorporating 'the revealing initiative of God
the Father, the redeeming work of God the Son, and the transforming
ministry of God the Holy Spirit' (1999: 28). This is a Trinitarian emphasis
supported by Alister McGrath (p. 88), Jürgen Moltmann (p. 109) and Loren
Wilkinson (p. 55). And as Stott points out, 'The evangelical faith reaches
beyond belief to behaviour; it brings with it a multifaceted challenge to live
accordingly' (1999: 135). This is where the *Declaration* supplies the factor
which O'Donovan failed to find – a hope which counteracts anxiety (p. 92).
The secular world sees little more than decay when it views creation;[4]
Christians see the same failures, but for them there is also the confident
hope that 'the universe itself is to be freed from the shackles of mortality ...
to enter upon the glorious liberty of the children of God' (Rom. 8:21, REB).
Our part is to accept and rejoice in God's work, and to be light for all the
world as obedient stewards.[5]

The God
who set the
stars in space

Timothy Dudley-Smith

Timothy Dudley-Smith is one of the leading hymn-writers of the present generation. He retired in 1992 after twelve years as Bishop of Thetford in the Anglican Diocese of Norwich, England. He has served as President of the Evangelical Alliance and of the Church of England Evangelical Council, and is the author of the definitive biography of John Stott.

The God who set the stars in space
    and gave the planets birth
created for our dwelling place
    a green and fruitful earth;
a world with wealth and beauty crowned
    of sky and sea and land,
where life should flourish and abound
    beneath its Maker's hand.

A world of order and delight
    God gave for us to tend,
to hold as precious in his sight,
    to nurture and defend;
but yet on ocean, earth and air
    the marks of sin are seen,
with all that God created fair
    polluted and unclean.

O God, by whose redeeming grace
    the lost may be restored,
who stooped to save our fallen race
    in Christ, creation's Lord,
through him whose cross is life and peace
    to cleanse a heart defiled
may human greed and conflict cease
    and all be reconciled.

Renew the wastes of earth again,
    redeem, restore, repair;
with us, your children, still maintain
    your covenant of care.
May we, who move from dust to dust
    and on your grace depend,
no longer, Lord, betray our trust
    but prove creation's friend.

Our God, who set the stars in space
    and gave the planets birth,
look down from heaven, your dwelling place,
    and heal the wounds of earth;
till pain, decay and bondage done,
    when death itself has died,
creation's songs shall rise as one
    and God be glorified!

86 86 D (DCM)

Suggested tune: ELLACOMBE or KINGSFOLD

Notes

Part I: Rationale

1. Callewaert (1994) lists sixty-three 'international documents [describing] the movement toward a global environmental ethic' (see also Bakken, Engel and Engel 1995). From the secular point of view, the most important are the Declarations of the UN Conference on the Human Environment and Development (Rio, 1991). In 1990 thirty-four well-known scientists led by Carl Sagan issued an 'Open Letter to the Religious Community', identifying the global environmental problems to be 'of such magnitude and solutions so broad, a perspective must be recognized from the outset as having a religious as well as a scientific dimension ... Efforts to safeguard and cherish the environment need to be infused with a vision of the sacred' (full text in Carroll and Warner 1998: ii–iii). Religious leaders (mainly from the US) responded the following year with a 'Statement at the Summit on Environment' (see Carroll and Warner 1998: vii–x). In 1992, 1,575 scientists signed 'The World's Scientists' Warning to Humanity' (see Ehrlich and Ehrlich 1996: 241–250). This was followed by a call for a 'global ethic' from the Parliament of the World's Religions which met in Chicago in 1993. This stated that

> By a global ethic we do not mean a single unified religion beyond all existing religions, and certainly not the domination of one religion over all others. By a global ethic we mean a fundamental consensus on binding values, irrevocable standards, and personal attitudes ... Earth cannot be changed for the better unless the consciousness of individuals is changed. We pledge to work for such transformation in individual and collective consciousness, for the awakening of our spiritual powers through reflection, meditation, prayer or positive thinking, for a conversion of the heart (Küng and Kuschel 1993: 21).

Many Christian assemblies have committed themselves to creation care. The Justice, Peace and the Integrity of Creation process is described on p. 28. The Anglican

187

Consultative Council made a formal statement to the UNCED organizers noting, on the basis of detailed studies by some of its provinces, that it espoused a common belief that

> All creation is of God and as part of creation we are given the specific tasks of responsible and faithful stewardship of all that is.
>
> This involves:
>
> (1) The clear understanding from both scripture and enduring tradition that:
>
> > (a) Responsible stewardship means that we are representative caretakers, managers or trustees, accountable for our actions;
> >
> > (b) The Christian gospel of reconciliation extends from 'a change from a level of human existence that is less than that envisaged by our Creator, to one in which humanity is fully human and free to move to a state of wholeness in harmony with God, with fellow human beings and with every aspect of his environment' (Statement of Sixth Meeting of the Anglican Consultative Council, 1987);
>
> (2) The misuse or misappropriation of the finite resources of the earth by ever increasing numbers of people is unsustainable, unjust and morally reprehensible;
>
> (3) Human dignity cannot be achieved or maintained in a degrading environment with a declining resource base. The traditional Christian aims of peace and justice must be supplemented by informed environmental care;
>
> (4) Environmental stewardship depends on the attitudes of individuals, corporations and governments. Because it involves maintaining the earth's sustainability for present and future allowing forbearance and fairness for all, current attitudes may have to change radically, particularly to manage actions with effects distant in time or place from their origin;
>
> (5) There is an encouraging convergence between the churches and secular bodies that stewardship is the basic ingredient for human survival and development, in the finite world in which we dwell. (Quoted in Berry 1992: 263–264.)

Successive Lambeth Conferences of Anglican bishops have commented on environmental problems. Lambeth X in 1968 inveighed against pollution. Lambeth XI in 1978 addressed an appeal to leaders and governments, conscious 'that time is running short'. Lambeth XII in 1988 called upon each province and diocese 'as a matter of urgency' to inform the faithful about 'what is happening to our environment and to see the stewardship of God's earth for the care of our neighbours as a necessary part of Christian discipleship'. Lambeth XIII (1998) set out an eco-theology under four headings: the creation covenant; the sacrament of creation; priests for creation; and the Sabbath feast of 'enoughness' (*Called to Full Humanity* 1999: 24ff.). The bishops prefaced their review:

> Plainly a great challenge and opportunity lies before the Church. Yet if that challenge is to be met, a widespread spiritual renewal and conversion must be experienced within the Church. There is also an urgent need for the Church to

reflect on Scripture and Christian tradition in the light of the ecological crisis and consequently to bring their faith into an effective engagement with the pursuit of a more sustainable way of life.

The gravity of the present challenge to the global ecosystem arises from the technologically enhanced impact of human intervention on our planet. Scripture was inspired in a different world but biblical insights into the nature of the God–human–world relation provide a firm foundation for a contemporary ecological theology.

Archbishop of Canterbury George Carey has stated that ecological challenges are 'unlikely to be met satisfactorily without the moral and spiritual motivation nurtured by the churches ... [But] our contributions to public debate about environmental responsibility have often been patchy and undistinguished' (Church House Seminar, October 1996).

Pope John Paul II has made a number of calls for creation care. On Earth Day 1990, he declared:

Since the ecological crisis is fundamentally a moral issue, it requires that all people respond in solidarity to what is a common threat. Uncontrolled exploitation of the natural environment not only menaces the survival of the human race, it also threatens the natural order in which mankind is meant to receive and to hand on God's gift of life with dignity and freedom. Today responsible men and women are increasingly aware that we must pay attention to what the earth and its atmosphere are telling us: namely, that there is an order in the universe which must be respected, and that the human person, endowed with the capability of choosing freely, has a grave responsibility to preserve this order for the well-being of future generations.

2. The original Au Sable Institute was established in the Great Lakes Forest, near Mancelona, north Michigan, in 1979 to serve as a centre for Christian environmental education. It has since extended to other centres: on an island in Puget Sound between Vancouver and Seattle and on Tangier Island in Chesapeake Bay, coastal Virginia; also in Tiruchirapalli, Tamil Nadu, India, and near Nairobi in Kenya. The Institute has sponsored a number of significant symposia on creation care (e.g. Granberg-Michaelson 1987; DeWitt 1991; DeWitt and Prance 1992).

3. The report 'Evangelical Christianity and the Environment' is published in full in *Transformation* (1992) 9.4: 27–30, and the *Evangelical Review of Theology* (1993) 17.2: 122–133. Other papers given at the Forum were also published in the *Review* 17.2, which was dedicated to 'Evangelicals and the environment: theological foundations for Christian environmental stewardship'. Further material from the Forum was published in *Transformation* (1993) 10.2.

4. Various Christian environmental organizations and denominational programmes have been active in the US since the 1980s. Their concerns gained greater visibility in 1993 with the formation of the National Religious Partnership for the Environment, an

outgrowth of the Joint Appeal in Science and Religion, which was an effort by scientists, senior religious leaders and politicians (including then-Senator Al Gore) to mobilize US religious communities on behalf of the environment. The Partnership comprises four major faith traditions: Jewish, Roman Catholic, mainline Protestant and evangelical. The evangelical community is addressed by the Evangelical Environment Network, a project of Evangelicals for Social Action. Like the other members of the Partnership, EEN develops its own materials and implements its own programmes with support from the Partnership.

Part II: Context

1. John Black traces the stewardship concept from Old Testament times. He quotes Sir Matthew Hale, Chief Justice of England, as making a particularly clear statement of stewardship in the introduction to *The Primitive Origination of Mankind* (1677). Towards the end of the book, he wrote:

> In relation therefore to this inferior World of Brutes and Vegetables, the End of Man's Creation was, that he should be the VICE-ROY of the great God of Heaven and Earth in this inferior World; his Steward, *Villicus*, Bayliff, or Farmer of this goodly Farm of the lower World, and reserved to himself the supreme Dominion, and the Tribute of Fidelity, Obedience, and Gratitude, as the greatest Recognition or Rent for the same, making his Usufructuary of this inferior World to husband and order it, and enjoy the Fruits thereof with sobriety, moderation, and thankfulness.
>
> And hereby Man was invested with power, authority, right, dominion, trust, and care, to correct and abridge the excesses and cruelties of the fiercer Animals, to give protection and defence to the mansuete and useful, to preserve the *Species* of divers Vegetables, to improve them and others, to correct the redundance of unprofitable Vegetables, to preserve the face of the Earth in beauty, usefulness, and fruitfulness. And surely, as it was not below the Wisdom and Goodness of God to create the very Vegetable Nature, and render the Earth more beautiful and useful by it, so neither was it unbecoming the same Wisdom to ordain and constitute such a subordinate Superintendent over it, that might take an immediate care of it.
>
> And certainly if we observe the special and peculiar accommodation and adaptation of Man, to the regiment and ordering of this lower World, we shall have reason, even without Revelation, to conclude that this was one End of the Creation of Man, namely, to be the Vice-gerent of Almighty God, in the subordinate Regiment especially of the Animal and Vegetable Provinces.

1. The historical roots of our ecologic crisis: Lynn White, Jr

1. This article was first printed in 1967. It is reprinted here with permission from *Science* 155: 1203–1207, with anglicizations. (Copyright 1967, American Association for the Advancement of Science.)

2. Biblical foundations for creation care: Ronald J. Sider

1. Parts of this chapter originally appeared in *Christianity Today*, 21 June 1993, and in *The Amicus Journal*, Spring 1995.

4. Creation's environmental challenge to evangelical Christianity: Calvin B. DeWitt

1. Modified from a paper published in the *Evangelical Review of Theology* (1993) 17: 134–149.

2. In the quotations on pp. 60 and 73 from the Geneva Bible (1560), archaic spellings have been modernized by the author.

3. One example and one citation only is presented for each of the seven degradations. The references cited in notes 2–9 are those given by DeWitt in his original paper. Further work has confirmed and strengthened the conclusions in his paper; the original references have been retained here to emphasize that the problems identified by DeWitt are not new and have been recognized in most cases for several decades. More comprehensive listings are available in Creation Watch Primer Sheets, available from Au Sable Outreach Office, 731 State Street, Madison, WI 53703, USA (phone +608–255–0950; fax +608–255–4228; email outreach@ausable.org. Other listings of the degradations are given by DeWitt in articles in *Perspectives on Science and Christian Faith* (1989) 41: 4–8, and *Firmament* (1990) 2: 5–9; *The Environment and the Christian* (ed. DeWitt): 13–23 (Grand Rapids, MI: Baker Book House, 1991); and *Earth-Wise*: 27–36 (Grand Rapids, MI: CRC Publications, 1994).

4. A specific example is ozone loss each spring over Antarctica, where twenty-five years of nearly continuous measurements by the British Antarctic Survey station at Halley Bay detected slight ozone decline, increasing in the late 1970s, with 30% depletion of the total column ozone content by 1984 and 70% in 1989 (Anderson, J., Toohey, D., and Brune, W., 'Free radicals within the Antarctic vortex: the role of CFCs in Antarctic ozone loss', *Science* [1991] 251: 39–461).

5. A specific example is that infiltration of rain water in eroded soils may be reduced by over 90%; in Zimbabwe water runoff is 20% to 30% greater than on non-eroded soil, with resulting water shortages even during years with good rainfall (Pimentel, D. T., et al., 'World agriculture and soil erosion', *BioScience* [1987] 37: 277–283).

6. A specific example is forest loss in Thailand, where forest cover declined from 29% to 19% of the land area between 1985 and 1988. In the Philippines, undisturbed forests have been reduced from 16 million hectares in 1960 to less than a million hectares at the time of writing (Repetto, R., 'Deforestation in the Tropics', *Scientific American* [April 1990]: 36–42).

7. A specific example is Ecuador, where since 1960 the original rainforest has been almost totally eliminated and converted to cash crops; a small remnant at Rio Palenque of less than one square kilometre is the only remaining site for forty-three plant species. The adjacent Centinella Ridge once supported 100 endemic plant species but was cleared between 1980 and 1984. (Given, D., 'Conserving botanical diversity on a global scale',

Annals of the Missouri Botanical Gardens [1990] 77: 48–62).

8. Between 5% and 10% of all wells examined in Europe and the US have nitrate levels higher than the recommended maximum of 45 milligrams per litre (Maurits la Rivière, J., 'Threats to the world's water', *Scientific American* [September 1989]: 80–94).

9. A specific example is the presence of DDT in the fatty tissue of penguins in Antarctica and the presence of pesticides in a remote lake on Isle Royale in Lake Superior between the United States and Canada – both extremely distant from the places where these materials are used.

10. A specific example is a 1975 study of the Hanunoo tribe of the Philippine Islands which found that an average adult could identify 1,600 different species – some 400 more than previously recorded in a systematic botanical survey; for Nigeria and elsewhere in the Two Thirds world there are similar findings (Awa, N., 'Participation and indigenous knowledge in rural development', *Knowledge* (1989) 10: 304–316).

11. A fuller treatment of the provisions of the biosphere can be found in DeWitt 1994: 11–24. Additional information, together with descriptions of environmental degradations and required responses, are given by Miller (1999) and Nebel and Wright (1999).

12. Saving people 'out of creation' has roots in the Platonic idea that physical nature is a source of ignorance and evil and is a snare to the soul, joined with the idea of human transcendence. This results in a theology which stresses salvation of the soul, dismissing as insignificant the body and the creation of which it was a part. The Bible does not make this distinction between the physical and the spiritual (Jeeves and Berry 1998; Brown, Murphy and Malony 1998). For a theological study of the importance of matter and of creation, and of the unbiblical hatred of creation by Marcion, and by Greek and Gnostic leaders, see Raymond C. Van Leeuwen, 'Christ's resurrection and the creation's vindication', in DeWitt 1991: 57–71.

13. These biblical principles have been published also in DeWitt 1994: 39–48.

Part III: Commentary

9. Stewardship and relationship: Richard Bauckham

1. In his *Song to David*, Christopher Smart (1722–70) wrote:

> The world, the clustering spheres, He made;
> The glorious light, the soothing shade,
> Dale, champaign, grove, and hill;
> The multitudinous abyss,
> Where Secrecy remains in bliss,
> And Wisdom hides her skill.
>
> Glorious the sun in mid career;
> Glorious th' assembled fires appear;
> Glorious the comet's train:
> Glorious the trumpet and alarm;

Glorious the Almighty's stretch'd-out arm;
Glorious th' enraptured main:

Glorious the northern lights astream;
Glorious the song, when God's the theme;
Glorious the thunder's roar:
Glorious Hosanna from the den;
Glorious the catholic Amen;
Glorious the martyr's gore:

Glorious – more glorious – is the crown
Of Him that brought salvation down,
By meekness call'd thy Son:
Thou that stupendous truth believed; –
And now the matchless deed's achieved,
Determined, dared, and done!

10. God's covenant and our responsibility: Jürgen Moltmann

1. Published in *Transformation* (April 1990) 7.1.

11. The Earth under threat: Ghillean T. Prance

1. From an analysis given after the Rio Earth Summit by Maurice Strong, Director-General of the UN Conference on Environment and Development, at the Fourth Kew Environmental Lecture.

18. Eschatology and hope: Ron Elsdon

1. 'It is the perspective from which the Church can encounter the typically modern experience of history as radical change in the direction of a new future, engage with possibilities for change, assess them in the light of the coming kingdom of God, and promote change in the direction of the kingdom' (Bauckham 1993: 385).

Part IV: Conclusions

1. The problem of seeking to learn moral lessons from the natural world is well illustrated by a letter from Charles Darwin to Asa Gray:

I own that I cannot see as plainly as others do, and as I should wish to do, evidence of design and beneficence on all sides of us. There seems to me too much misery in the world. I cannot persuade myself that a beneficent and omnipotent God would have designedly created the Ichneumonidae with the express intention of their feeding within the living bodies of Caterpillars, or that a cat should play with mice.

This is quoted by Gould (1983: 41), discussing the futility of trying to discern ethical messages from natural processes.

2. The time factor is 'the Achilles' heel of natural theology'. Mayr (1982: 49) says:

> It would be possible for a creator to design a perfect organism in a static world of short duration. However, how could species have remained perfectly adapted to their environment if this environment was constantly changing, and sometimes quite drastically? How could design have foreseen all the changes of climate, of the physical structure of the surface of the earth, and of the changing composition of ecosystems (predators and competitors) if the earth was hundreds of millions of years old? Adaptations under these circumstances can be maintained only if the organisms constantly adjust themselves to the new circumstances, that is, if they evolve. Although the natural theologians, good naturalists that they were, had clearly recognized the importance of the environment and the adaptations of organisms to it, they had failed to take the time factor into consideration. Lamarck was the first to have clearly recognized the crucial importance of this factor'.

3. 'Darwinism appeared, and, under the disguise of a foe, did the work of a friend. It has conferred upon philosophy and religion an inestimable benefit, by showing us that we must choose between two alternatives. Either God is everywhere present in nature, or He is nowhere.'

4. This is encapsulated by the so-called Fifth Gospel, repeatedly quoted in 'green' writings and allegedly propounded by the American Indian Chief Seattle in the 1850s, but which is now known to have been written by an American film-writer in 1971, based (as far as can be ascertained) on a much more gloomy original, 'The Indian's Night Promised to be Dark' (Editor, 1989). Native wisdom can be informative, but it may be nothing more than common sense in a particular situation.

5. The difficulties in modern evangelical response to social demands are well illustrated by the debates around the Lausanne Declaration (Chester 1993).

Bibliography

Aeschliman, G. (1994), 'Somebody got shot in the head', *Prism* (December/January), p. 7.

Assisi Declarations (1986), 'Messages on man and nature', Gland, Switzerland: Worldwide Fund for Nature.

Attfield, R. (1991), *The Ethics of Environmental Concern* (second edition), Athens, GA: University of Georgia Press.

—— (1999), *The Ethics of the Global Environment*, Edinburgh: Edinburgh University Press.

Bakken, P. W., Engel, J. G., and Engel, J. R. (1995), *Ecology, Justice and Christian Faith: A Critical Guide to the Literature*, Westport, CT: Greenwood Press.

Barr, J. (1968), 'The image of God in the book of Genesis: a study of terminology', *Bulletin of the John Rylands Library* 51: 11 – 26.

Bauckham, R. (1993), 'Moltmann, Jürgen', in McGrath, A. E. (ed.), *The Blackwell Encyclopaedia of Modern Christian Thought*: 385–388, Oxford: Blackwell.

Begbie, J. (1991), *Voicing Creation's Praise: Towards a Theology of the Arts*, Edinburgh: T. & T. Clark.

Beisner, E. C. (1990), *Prospects for Growth*, Westchester, IL: Crossway.

—— (1993), 'Are God's resources finite?' *World* (27 November): 10–13.

—— (1997), *Where Garden Meets Wilderness*, Grand Rapids, MI: Eerdmans.

—— (1998), 'Putting Kyoto on ice', *World* (8 August): 12–16.

Berry, R. J. (ed.) (1992), *Environmental Dilemmas*, London: Chapman & Hall.

—— (1995), 'Creation and the environment', *Science and Christian Belief* 7: 21–43.

—— (1999), 'Christian approach to the environment', *Transformation* 16. 3: 73–74.

Birch, C., Eakin, W., and McDaniel, J. B. (eds.) (1998), *Liberating Life*, Maryknoll, NY: Orbis.

Black, J. (1970), *The Dominion of Man*, Edinburgh: Edinburgh University Press.

Blocher, H. (1984), *In the Beginning*, Leicester: IVP.

—— (1997), *Original Sin*, Leicester: Apollos.

Bomer, N. (1993a), 'Assault on jobs: Regulation, however intended, is getting a chokehold', *World* (4 September): 22–23.

—— (1993b), 'Out of balance: Green agenda is putting loggers on the endangered list', *World* (20 March): 33.

Bouma-Prediger, S. (1995), *The Greening of Theology*, Atlanta, GA: Scholars Press.

—— (1997), 'Creation as the home of God: the doctrine of creation in the theology of Jürgen Moltmann', *Calvin Theological Journal* 32: 72–90.

Bratton, S. P. (1992), *Six Billion and More*, Louisville, KN: Westminster/John Knox Press.

Brenton, T. (1994), *The Greening of Machiavelli*, London: Earthscan.

Brooke, G. J. (1987), 'Creation in the biblical tradition', *Zygon* 22: 227–248.

Brown, W. S., Murphy, N., and Malony, H. N. (eds.) (1998), *Whatever Happened to the Soul?* Minneapolis, MN: Fortress.

Buckland, W. (1837), *Geology and Mineralogy Considered with Reference to Natural Theology*, London: William Pickering.

Bush, R. B., and Folger, J. P. (1994), *The Promise of Mediation: Responding to Conflict through Empowerment and Recognition*, San Francisco: Jossey-Bass.

Called to Full Humanity (1999), Lambeth Conference 1998: Section I, Harrisburg, PA: Morehouse.

Callewaert, J. H. (1994), *International Documents and the Movement toward a Global Environmental Ethic* (circulated at the International Union for the Conservation of Nature Congress, Buenos Aires).

Campolo, T. (1992), *How to Rescue the Earth without Worshipping Nature*, Nashville, TN: Thomas Nelson.

Caring for the Earth (1991) (revision of the World Conservation Strategy),

Gland, Switzerland: International Union for the Conservation of Nature, Worldwide Fund for Nature, United Nations Environmental Programme.

Carroll, J. E., and Warner, K. (eds.) (1998), *Ecology and Religion: Scientists Speak*, Quincey, IL: Franciscan Press.

Chester, T. (1993), *Awakening to a World of Need*, Leicester: IVP.

Cobb, J. B. (1972), *Is It Too Late?*, Beverly Hills, CA: Bruce.

—— (1992), *Sustainability: Economics, Ecology and Justice*, Maryknoll, NY: Orbis.

Cohen, J. (1989), *'Be Fertile and Increase, Fill the Earth and Master It': The Ancient and Medieval Career of a Biblical Text*, Ithaca, NY: Cornell University Press.

Cohen, J. E. (1995), *How Many People Can the Earth Support?* New York: W. W. Norton.

Cranfield, C. E. B. (1974), 'Some observations on Romans 8:19–21', in Banks, R. (ed.), *Reconciliation and Hope: New Testament Essays on Atonement and Eschatology presented to L. L. Morris on his 60th birthday*: 224–230. Grand Rapids, MI: Eerdmans.

Craston, C. (1992), 'Reflections on Canberra 1991', *Anvil* 9: 27–38.

DeWitt, C. B. (ed.) (1991), *The Environment and the Christian*, Grand Rapids, MI: Baker Book House.

—— (1993), 'God's love for the world', *Evangelical Review of Theology* 17: 134–149.

—— (1994), *Earthwise*, Grand Rapids, MI: CRC Publishing.

—— (1995), 'Ecology and ethics: Relation of religious belief to ecological practice in the biblical tradition', *Biodiversity and Conservation* 4: 838–848.

—— (1998), *Caring for Creation*, Grand Rapids, MI: Baker Book House.

—— and Prance, G. T. (eds.) (1992), *Missionary Earthkeeping*, Macon, GA: Mercer University Press.

Dowd, M. (1991), *Earthspirit*, Mystic, CT: Twenty-Third Publications.

Dunn, J. (1988), *Romans 1 - 8*, Word Biblical Commentary, Waco, TX: Word.

Edinburgh, HRH The Duke of, and Mann, M. (1989), *Survival or Extinction: A Christian Attitude to the Environment*, Windsor Castle: Michael Russell.

Editor, The (1989), 'The gospel of Chief Seattle is a hoax', *Environmental Ethics* 11: 195–196.

Ehrlich, P. R., and Ehrlich, A. H. (1996), *Betrayal of Science and Reason: How*

Anti-environmental Rhetoric Threatens our Future, Washington, DC: Island Press.

Elsdon, R. (1992), *Greenhouse Theology*, Tunbridge Wells: Monarch.

Ferguson, S. B., and Wright, D. F. (eds.) (1988), *New Dictionary of Theology*, Leicester: IVP.

Fergusson, D. A. S. (1998), *The Cosmos and the Creator*, London: SPCK.

Finger, T. (1998), *Evangelicals, Eschatology and the Environment*, Wynne-wood, PA: Evangelical Environmental Network.

Forsyth, P. T. (1997), *The Soul of Prayer* (reprint), Vancouver, BC: Regent College Publishing.

Fowler, R. B. (1995), *The Greening of Protestant Thought*, Chapel Hill, NC: University of North Carolina Press.

Gelbspan, R. (1998), *The Heat is On* (revised edition), Reading, MA: Perseus.

Gilkey, L. (1959), *Maker of Heaven and Earth: The Christian Doctrine of Creation in the Light of Modern Knowledge*, Garden City, NY: Doubleday.

Glacken, C. J. (1967), *Traces on the Rhodian Shore: Nature and Culture in Western Thought from Ancient Times to the End of the Eighteenth Century*, Berkeley, CA: University of California Press.

Gore, A. (1992), *Earth in the Balance*, Boston: Houghton Mifflin.

Gosling, D. L. (1992), *A New Earth: Covenanting for Justice, Peace and the Integrity of Creation*, London: Council of Churches of Britain and Ireland.

Gould, S. J. (1983), 'Non-moral nature', in *Hen's Teeth and Horse's Toes*: 30–45. New York: W. W. Norton.

Granberg-Michaelson, W. (ed.) (1987), *Tending the Garden*, Grand Rapids, MI: Eerdmans.

Green, L. W., George, M. A., Daniel, M., Frankish, C. J., Herbert, C. P., Bowie, W. R., and O'Neil, M. (1995), 'Background on participatory research', in *Study of Participatory Research in Health Promotion in Canada*, Royal Society of Canada.

Grove-White, R. (1992), 'Human identity and the environmental crisis', in Ball, J., Goodall, M., Palmer, C., and Reader, J. (eds.), *The Earth Beneath*: 13–34. London: SPCK.

Guillebaud, J. (1995), 'After Cairo', *British Journal of Obstetrics and Gynaecology* 102: 436–438.

—— (1996), 'After Cairo (correspondence)', *British Journal of Obstetrics and Gynaecology* 103: 92–93.

Gunton, C. (1991), *The Promise of Trinitarian Theology*, Edinburgh: T. & T. Clark.

Hall, D. J. (1986), *Imaging God: Dominion as Stewardship*, Grand Rapids, MI: Eerdmans.

Hamilton, L. S. (ed.) (1993), *Ethics, Religion and Bio-diversity*, Cambridge: White Horse Press.

Hartleib, E. (1996), *Natur als Schöpfung: Studien zum Verhältnis von Naturbegriff und Schöpfungverständnis bei Günter Altner, Sigurd M. Daecke, Hermann Dembowski und Christian Link*, Frankfurt am Main: Peter Lang.

Hinsdale, M. A., Lewis, H. M., and Waller, S. M. (1995), *It Comes from the People: Community Development and Local Theology*, Philadelphia: Temple University Press.

Hopes and Realities: Closing the Gap between Women's Aspirations and their Reproductive Experiences (1995), New York: Alan Guttmacher Institute.

Houghton, J. T. (1988), *Does God Play Dice?* Leicester: IVP.

—— (1994), *Global Warming*, Oxford: Lion.

—— (1995), *The Search for God: Can Science Help?* Oxford: Lion.

Jeeves, M. A., and Berry, R. J. (1998), *Science, Life and Christian Belief*, Leicester: Apollos.

Kidner, D. (1967), *Genesis*, Tyndale Old Testament Commentary, London: Tyndale.

Küng, H. (1991), *Global Responsibility: In Search of a New World Ethic*, New York: Crossroad.

—— and Kuschel, K.-J. (eds.) (1993), *A Global Ethic: The Declaration of the Parliament of the World's Religions*, London: SCM.

La Cugna, C. M. (1993), *God for Us: The Trinity and Christian Life*, San Francisco: HarperCollins.

Leslie, J. (1993), 'Creation stories, religious and atheistic', *International Journal for Philosophy of Religion* 34: 67–77.

Lewis, L. M. (1992), *The Promethean Politics of Milton, Blake and Shelley*, London: University of Missouri Press.

Lloyd-Jones, D. M. (1975), *Romans: An Exposition of Chapter 8:17–39*, Edinburgh: Banner of Truth.

Lohfink, N. (1994), 'God the Creator and the stability of heaven and earth: The Old Testament on the connection between creation and salvation', in Lohfink, N. (ed.), *Theology of the Pentateuch*: 116–135, Edinburgh: T. & T. Clark.

Lovelock, J. E. (1979), *Gaia: A New Look at Life on Earth*, Oxford: Oxford University Press.

—— (1988), *The Ages of Gaia*, Oxford: Oxford University Press.

McGrath, A. E. (1998), *The Foundations of Dialogue in Science and Religion*, Oxford: Blackwell.

McHarg, I. L. (1969), *Design with Nature*, New York: Natural History.

McMichael, A. J., and Powles, J. W. (1999), 'Human numbers, environment, sustainability and health', *British Medical Journal* 319: 977–980.

Manahan, R. (1991), 'Christ as the second Adam', in DeWitt, C. B. (ed.), *The Environment and the Christian*: 45–56, Grand Rapids, MI: Eerdmans.

Maser, Chris (1996), *Resolving Environmental Conflict: Towards a Sustainable Community Development*, Delray Beach, FL: St Lucie Press.

May, G. (1995), *Creation Ex Nihilo*, Edinburgh: T. & T. Clark.

Mayr, E. (1982), *The Growth of Biological Thought*, Cambridge, MA: Harvard University Press.

Miller, G. T. (1999), *Living in the Environment* (eleventh edition), Belmont, CA: Wadsworth.

Mission in a Broken World (1990), Report of ACC-8 Wales, London: Church Publishing House.

Moltmann, J. (1985), *God in Creation*, London: SCM.

Montefiore, H. (1969), *The Question Mark*, London: Collins.

—— (ed.) (1975), *God and Nature*, London: Collins.

Moo, D. (1996), *Epistle to the Romans*, New International Commentary on the New Testament, Grand Rapids, MI: Eerdmans.

Moore, A. (1889), 'The Christian doctrine of God', in Gore, C. (ed.), *Lux Mundi* (tenth edition), London: John Murray.

Moule, C. F. D. (1964), *Man and Nature in the New Testament*, London: Athlone.

Moule, H. C. G. (1879), *Romans*, Cambridge: Cambridge University Press.

Naess, A. (1989), *Ecology, Community and Lifestyle*, Cambridge: Cambridge University Press.

Napier, B. D. (1962), 'On Creation-faith in the Old Testament', *Interpretation* 16: 21–42.

Nash, J. (1992), *Loving Nature: Ecological Integrity and Christian Responsibility*, Nashville, TN: Abingdon.

Nebel, B. J., and Wright, R. T. (1999), *Environmental Science* (seventh edition), Englewood Cliffs, NJ: Prentice Hall.

Nicholson, E. M. (1970), *The Environmental Revolution*, London: Hodder & Stoughton.

—— (1987), *The New Environmental Age*, Cambridge: Cambridge University Press.

Niles, D. P. (ed.) (1992), *Between the Flood and the Rainbow*, Geneva: World Council of Churches.

Noll, M. (1994), *The Scandal of the Evangelical Mind*, Leicester: IVP.

Northcott, M. S. (1996), *The Environment and Christian Ethics*, Cambridge: Cambridge University Press.

—— (1999), *Life After Debt*, London: SPCK.

O'Brien, P. T. (1982), *Colossians and Philemon*, Word Biblical Commentary, Waco, TX: Word.

O'Donovan, O. (1986), *Resurrection and Moral Order: An Outline for Evangelical Ethics* (second edition 1994), Leicester: Apollos.

Oelschlaeger, M. (1994), *Caring for Creation: An Ecumenical Approach to the Environmental Crisis*, New Haven, CN: Yale University Press.

O'Hear, A. (1997), *NonSense about Nature*, London: Social Affairs Unit.

Our Common Future (1987), Report of the World Commission on Environment and Development (the Brundtland Report), New York: Oxford University Press.

Palmer, C. (1992), 'Stewardship: A case study in environmental ethics', in Ball, I., Goodall, M., Palmer, C., and Reader, J. (eds.), *The Earth Beneath*: 67–86. London: SPCK.

Polanyi, M. (1962), *Personal Knowledge*, London: Routledge & Kegan Paul.

Polkinghorne, J. (1988), *Science and Creation*, London: SPCK.

Prance, G. T. (1996), *Earth under Threat*, Glasgow: Wild Goose.

Preuss, H. D. (1995), *Old Testament Theology*, Louisville, KY: John Knox Press.

Prins, G. (ed.) (1993), *Threats without Enemies*, London: Earthscan.

Rothschild, B., and Martin, L. (1993), *Paleopathology: Disease in the Fossil Record*, London: CRC Press.

Santmire, P. (1985), *The Travail of Nature*, Philadelphia, PA: Fortress.

Schader-Frechette, R. S. (1981), *Environmental Ethics*, Pacific Grove, CA: Boxwood.

Schaeffer, F. A. (1970), *Pollution and the Death of Man*, London: Hodder & Stoughton.

Seaton, C. (1992). *Whose Earth?* London: Crossway.

Setting Environmental Standards (1998), Twenty-first Report of the Royal

Commission on Environmental Pollution, London: Stationery Office.

Sheldon, J. K. (1989), 'Twenty-one years after the "Historical roots of our ecologic crisis": How has the church responded?' *Perspectives on Science and Christian Faith* 41: 152–158.

—— (1992), *Rediscovery of Creation: A Bibliographical Study of the Church's Response to the Environmental Crisis*, Metuchen, NJ: Scarecrow Press.

Sider, R. J. (1978), *Rich Christians in an Age of Hunger*, Downers Grove, IL: IVP.

—— (1990), 'Reflections on Justice, Peace and the Integrity of Creation', *Transformation* 7: 15–17.

—— (1994), 'Another view', *World* (8 January): 22–24.

Strong, M. (1993), The Fourth Kew Environmental Lecture, London: Royal Botanic Gardens.

Sugden, C. (1990), 'The poor are the losers', *Transformation* 7: 18–19.

—— (1993), 'Evangelicals and environment in process', *Evangelical Review of Theology* 17: 119–121.

Suzuki, D. (1997), *The Sacred Balance: Rediscovering our Place in Nature*, Vancouver: Greystone Books.

This Common Inheritance (1990), White Paper on the environment, London: HMSO. Cm. 1200.

Thompson, P. E. S. (1971), 'The Yahwist creation story', *Vetus Testamentum* 21: 197–208.

Trousson, R. (1976), *La Thème de Prométhée dans la Litérature Européene*, Geneva: Droz.

US National Academy of Sciences (1993), *Population Summit of the World's Scientific Academies, New Delhi*, Washington: US National Academy.

Van Bavel, T. (1990), 'The Creator and the integrity of creation in the Fathers of the Church', *Augustinian Studies* 21: 1–33.

Van Till, H. J. (1996), 'Basil, Augustine and the doctrine of creation's functional integrity', *Science and Christian Belief* 8: 21–38.

Wenham, G. J. (1987), *Genesis 1 – 15*, Word Biblical Commentary, Waco, TX: Word.

Westermann, C. (1971), *Creation*, London: SPCK.

Whelan, R., Kirwan, J., and Haffner, P. (1996), *The Cross and the Rain Forest*, Grand Rapids, MI: Eerdmans.

White, L. (1967), 'The historical roots of our ecologic crisis', *Science* 155: 1203–1207.

Whitney, E. (1993), 'Lynn White, ecotheology and history', *Environmental Ethics* 15: 151–169.

Wilkinson, L. (ed.) (1990), *Earth-keeping in the Nineties*, Grand Rapids, MI: Eerdmans. (Second edition of *Earth-keeping*, 1980.)

Wilson, E. O. (1998), *Consilience*, New York: Alfred Knopf.

World Conservation Strategy (1980), Gland, Switzerland: International Union for the Conservation of Nature, Worldwide Fund for Nature, United Nations Environmental Programme.

Wright, R. T. (1995), 'Tearing down the green: environmental backlash in the evangelical subculture', *Perspectives on Science and Christian Faith* 47: 80–91.

Zerbe, G. (1991), 'The kingdom of God and stewardship of creation', in *The Environment and the Christian*: 73–92, Grand Rapids, MI: Eerdmans.

The John Ray Initiative

The John Ray Initiative is a charity dedicated to promoting responsible environmental stewardship in accordance with Christian principles and the wise use of science and technology. All royalties from sales of this book are being given to this Initiative.

The John Ray Initiative was launched in 1997 with the objectives:

- to demonstrate and teach the wonder of nature, including its diversity and complexity
- to increase awareness of environmental harm (e.g. pollution, biodiversity loss, climate change) resulting from our failure to be good stewards
- to encourage responsible stewardship and stimulate the development of a Christian understanding of the environment and the way in which human society interacts within it
- to demonstrate and teach how the natural and social sciences and technology can be harnessed to protect the environment and ameliorate environmental damage
- to stimulate action locally, nationally and internationally, in pursuit of environmental protection and sustainable development
- to encourage and cooperate with Christian environmental initiatives and those of other relevant organizations
- to demonstrate good environmental stewardship

The Patrons of the John Ray Initiative include the Archbishop of Canterbury, Professor Calvin DeWitt, Sir Ghillean Prance, FRS, and the

Revd John Stott. The Chairman is Sir John Houghton, FRS.

The office of the Initiative is based in the Cheltenham and Gloucester College of Higher Education, Francis Close Hall, Swindon Road, Cheltenham, Gloucestershire GL50 4AZ.

Internet: www.jri.org.uk *Email*: jri@jchelt.ac.uk

Information on and contact details of other Christian environmental organizations can be provided by the John Ray Initiative office.

General index

Index of Bible references